ARIZONA Chefs

Dine-In Dine-Out COOK BOOK

Compiled and
written by
Elin Jeffords
with 35 of
Arizona's
Leading Chefs

Dine-In Dine-Out COOK BOOK

Arizona Chefs
Dine-In/Dine-Out CookBook
is published annually
by Horizon Media,
4710 N. 16th Street, Suite 102,
Phoenix, Arizona 85016.
Phone: (602) 248-8323.

Staff

Publisher
Ron Kindsfater

Editor
Elin Jeffords

Photographer
John Ormond

Graphic Designer
Randy Galloway

Offset Lithography
Paragon Printing

ISBN 0-9659883-0-9

Dine-In Dine-Out COOK BOOK

Acknowledgements

Much appreciation to Ron Kindsfater for coming up with the basic idea for the book and his non-stop can-do attitude in getting it off the ground. Thanks to John Ormond for his tireless pursuit of the perfect photo. Randy Galloway deserves appreciation for creating the striking design and graphics. I also want to thank the many chefs, owners and PR people who cooperated in putting their parts of the book together and burying me in fax paper for three months. Special thanks to Patrick Hughes for his cover photo cactus entree and recipe. And as always, thanks to Phil Allen for his on-going support and peerless computer skills.

Dine-In Dine-Out COOK BOOK

CONTENTS

Dine-In
Dine-Out
COOK
BOOK

C
O
N
T
E
N
T
S

Welcome to The Arizona Chefs Dine In - Dine Out Cookbook. With it in hand you will be able to duplicate the recipes of top chefs from around the state. You will also have the opportunity to visit their restaurants and use a gift certificate from the back of the book that will give you a $10 discount off your meal (and the chance to see how your rendition of the chef's dish stacks up the real thing).

Here is how to get the very best out of the book. We've sub-titled it "Entertaining with Restaurant Flair" and designed it so that it can be accessed for everything from a casual barbecue to an elegant soup-to-nuts dinner party. You put just as much, or as little, effort into the meal as you desire.

To digress slightly, it has never before been easier to enter-tain. I often hear people say, "I'd love to entertain more. I just dread the chore of cooking." Not an excuse anymore. With all the excellent pre-prepared and convenience items on the market, the average home cook can put together a Martha Stewart-esque spread with very little effort.

My husband and I entertain frequently - sometimes four or five times a month. Our trick for keeping it a joy rather than a hardship is putting effort into only one or two of the dishes we serve and filling in with crackers and bought spreads, salads based on bagged mixes, easy sides like polenta and couscous and then, ending up with bakery cookies or interesting cheeses and fresh fruit. If we want to make an elaborate appetizer and\or dessert, we keep the main dish very simple. Remember, guests are joining you not to critique your efforts, they are there to enjoy good company and a good time. (For some of my favorite cooking tips, please see pages 8 and 9.)

Though each participating restaurant and chef has contributed four recipes, they aren't necessarily intended to be prepared together—though they can be. For instance, Baby Kay's Lagniappe Salad and Barbecued Shrimp along with crusty store-bought bread and lemon pie will have guests in heaven. For a weekend dinner on the patio, grill up Manuel's Fish Tacos and make their super-easy, super-good Skillet Apple Pie ala Mode. With bagged lettuce mix and tomato salad, you're all set. When weather is cool, try Smoked Corn with Sunflower Sprouts soup and Tinga Poblana, both from chef Patrick Hughes. Warm, buttered corn tortillas and coleslaw make it a festive and complete meal. You get the picture.

You can also mix and match among the restaurants recipes. Make the simple but wonderfully crunchy and tasty Wedge of Iceburg from Tarbell's along with Tenderloin Tower with Ricotta Gnocchi from Aldo Baldo. Pair Scott Uehlein's Spicy Beef Salad with RoxSand's Blueberry Tart with Ginger Ice Cream. Try Franco's Risotto Funghi Porcini preceded by Stracciatella soup from Gianni's. Multiple and mouthwatering combinations are possible.

For occasions when time is not an issue and a relaxed day in the kitchen can serve as personal therapy as well as resulting in a show stopper dinner, we have more elaborate options such as Jeff Beeson's Pork Tenderloin Marinated in Dark Beer with Candied Nectarine and Onion Sauce and Creamy Yellow Grits, or Doctor Bombay's Calcutta Feast from Team A.J.'s.

Consider, too, deconstructing some of the recipe combinations—preparing just the Creamy Grits along with grilled sausages or using the Braised Lentil Ragout from Doctor Bombay's Feast with your own curry-dusted pork chops.

Finally, many of the recipes are simple and quick enough to make for a busy day family dinner—Anton Brunbauer's Southwest Shrimp Caesar Salad, Mostaciolli with Brocolli and Sundried Tomatoes from Michelina Disibio and Linda Rose's Pork Chops with Cherry Peppers to name just a few.

John Ormond's full color photographs of all the dishes give you a blueprint for presentation. All recipes serve four and can easily be doubled. As with any new recipe, read it through carefully before you start cooking. Ingredients are listed in order used. If there are several parts to the recipe, they are arranged so that they may be prepared in sequence.

The chefs shared their beverage recommendations with us, but naturally you know best what you and your guests most enjoy. As a little extra, we've also included some of the chefs favorite kitchen tips.

I've had a lot of fun putting this book together and think I can promise that you will enjoy using it.

Elin Entertains

As I stated in the introduction, my style of entertaining is to take full advantage of all the terrific pre-prepared food available. I save my energy for one or two labor-intensive courses and sometimes, I don't even do that. Here are some of my quick and effective meal tricks.

Appetizers

* Cream room temperature Gorgonzola with a little olive oil and a generous grind of black pepper and spread into celery stalks.

* When tomatoes are red and ripe, squeeze out seeds, chop coarsely and combine with chopped basil, chopped garlic, a little olive oil and salt and pepper. Let sit about 20 minutes so flavors blend. Heap on toasted Italian bread for Bruschetta (also makes an excellent pasta sauce).

* When you are grilling outdoors, roast a few heads of garlic. (Peel excess husk but keep head together. Cut off top fourth of head. Dribble on a little olive oil, wrap in foil and cook on the grill about 45 minutes or until soft.) It is delicious squeezed warm on chewy bread or toast. Save any left over to add a distinctive but mild flavor to other dishes such as sauteed spinach, pasta sauces and mashed potatoes.

* Drain and coarsely puree a can of small white beans with about a half dozen cloves of roasted garlic, a dribble of olive oil, a tablespoon of fresh rosemary and salt and pepper. Serve with crackers and crudites.

* Drain and rinse a can of black beans, a can of small white corn kernels and combine with a drained can of chopped green chiles. Add some chopped red onion, a squirt of tabasco, cumin, oregano and salt and pepper to taste. Serve with tortilla chips.

* This works with both eggplant and bell peppers - slice eggplant and grill until brown and softened. Grill peppers until skin starts to blacken, place in paper bag to "sweat", then peel and carefully cut in half and remove seeds. While veggies are cooling, cream room temperature goat cheese (you can add chopped fresh herbs such as oregano and basil if you wish). Spoon cheese into center of eggplant and peppers and roll up. Dress with good olive oil and balsamic vinegar. (Also makes a nice salad placed on greens.)

Salads

I'm a big believer in bagged mixes, the time and waste they save is well worth the cost.

* With butter lettuce and radicchio, add sliced and cored ripe pears, a generous sprinkle of blue cheese and toasted walnuts or pinons with your favorite vinaigrette.

* With the "Italian" mix, add roasted red pepper strips, red onion and black olives with a zesty italian dressing.

* Feta, cucumbers and tomatoes and a generous amount of oregano turns iceburg into a Greek salad.

* This is an original that may sound weird but everyone loves it. Wash and dry

1 large head of curly endive. Slice finely the long way across the leaves and place in a large bowl. Meanwhile, fry about 10 slices of bacon until very crisp. Set aside. Reserve a scant 1/2 cup bacon grease and add 2 tablespoons red wine vinegar and a generous squirt of Tabasco. Heat in microwave until boiling and pour over lettuce. Toss and cover for about 10 minutes. Just before serving add a can of drained and rinsed black eyed peas, 1/4 pound crumbled blue cheese and the crumbled bacon and toss again with lots of fresh ground black pepper. Serve with Cajun seasoning-rubbed grilled steak and garlic toast.

Entrees

* Since we went to Spain, my husband has become a paella-meister. It is one of those dishes that takes some organization as far as gathering and prepping the ingredients, but it goes together in a snap. One of the other beauties of paella is you can add virtually anything; onions, peppers, peas, seafood, chicken, pork, sausage, even escargot.

* Butterflied, marinated and grilled leg of lamb is a one of those no-fail main dishes (as long as it is not over-cooked). We usually marinate it in pomegranate juice (available in health food and Middle-eastern stores) with garlic, rosemary and olive oil. Serve with rice pilaf or garlic mashed potatoes (boil the garlic right along with the potatoes or use roasted garlic).

* Both Trader Joe's and Cost Plus have dried mushrooms. I reconstitute them in warm water with a little sherry and make a pasta sauce with shallots sauteed in olive oil, the lightly drained mushrooms and heavy cream, reduced slightly. With a good grated parmesan, it is simply luxurious.

* Another simple and luxurious treat is hot off the grill steaks heaped with melting gorgonzola and grilled onion rings.

* Grilled turkey breast goes uptown when you make a puree out of fresh herbs, garlic, a little olive oil and salt and pepper and slip it under the skin of the breast. It keeps the meat moist and flavorful and looks gorgeous when it is sliced. This also works well with a whole butterflied chicken.

* I make posole using canned hominy, red enchilada sauce and chicken broth with grilled chicken breasts or leftover pork roast. Use lots of oregano and serve with shredded cabbage, sliced radishes, sliced avocados and limes for garnish. With hot quesadilla wedges and a fruit salad for dessert it is a festive meal that takes literally not much more than an hour to assemble.

Desserts

I am not a baker, it takes too much patience and there are all kinds of ready-mades out there that need little, if any, dressing up.

* In the fall, I buy frozen pumpkin pies when they are on sale and then make a topping out of brown sugar, butter and pecans. Browned under the broiler it looks and tastes great especially with bourbon-flavored whipped cream

* Costco carries a great little lemon-poppy seed bundt cake. I take a bag of frozen blueberries and reduce them to a sauce to serve along with it.

* Fruit and bakery brownies or cookies are always good.

Remember - successful entertaining is not about exhausting yourself in the kitchen, it is about having fun, not only your guests - but you, too!

A.J.'s

Gary LeBarge II and Michael Whelan
Chefs

Valley cooks worth their respective salts know that for quality ingredients A.J.'s is the only place to go. This is kitchen headquarters for fabulous cheeses, exotic produce, fine meats and seafood, quality bakery and all those off-beat ingredients that are simply impossible to find anywhere else in town.

Plenty of folks who DON'T cook, frequent A.J.'s as well. They are the ones heading for Treat's Deli. That Deli designation doesn't begin to tell the story of all the goodies chefs LeBarge and Whelan prepare for take-out each day.

Literally thousands of customers rely on A.J.'s for their holiday meals and catering is also a major chunk of Treat's business.

It takes a special kind of chef to handle this kind of load, and Whelan and LeBarge both have excellent credentials. Whelan came to A.J's from Mary Elaine's at The Phoenician and has worked in hospitality venues from Maryland to Hawaii. He credits his father for imparting to him the philosophy that it is important to do what you love and not be concerned with material rewards.

A strong parental influence, in this case the encouragement of his mother, also started LeBarge on his chosen path. He came to A.J.'s from The Wigwam and frequently involves himself in culinary benefits such as ZooFari.

A.J.'s:
7141 E. Lincoln Dr., Scottsdale. 998-0052
10105 E. Via Linda, Scottsdale. 391-9863
5017 N. Central Ave., Phoenix. 230-7015
13226 N. 7th St., Phoenix. 863-3500
23251 N. Pima Rd., Scottsdale. 563-5070

Banana Radish Salad
with Orange Vinagrette

Salad

3 medium bananas, cut in 1 inch slices
4 large radishes, sliced thin and then
    cut into matchsticks
1/2 cup mandarin orange segments

1/2 cup orange juice
1/4 cup salad oil
1/4 cup mint, coarsely chopped
4 mint sprigs (garnish)

Toss all ingredients together in a mixing bowl, making sure they are well-incorporated. Place on 4 chilled plates and garnish with mint sprigs.

*Beverage recommendation - Gewurztraminer.

Cracked Black Peppercorn Crusted
Pork Loin with Pommery Mustard Sauce

Entree

2 pounds pork loin
2 tablespoons cracked black pepper
salt to taste

mustard sauce (see recipe below)
vegetable ragout (see recipe below)

Preheat oven to 350° Coat pork with pepper and salt. Sear in a saute pan until golden brown on all sides. Transfer pork to a baking dish and finish cooking for about 25 minutes or until 140° internal temperature. Remove from oven and let sit about 10 minutes.

Mustard Sauce

1/2 cup dry white wine
1/2 cup chicken broth
1 stalk celery, chopped

5 small whole white mushrooms
1 - 1/2 tablespoons Pommery or whole grain mustard
2 cups heavy cream

In a medium saucepot combine first 5 ingredients. Place on medium high heat and reduce liquid until almost dry. Add cream and reduce again by 1/3 or to a sauce consistency. Keep warm

Vegetable Ragout

2 tablespoons olive oil
8 red Bliss potatoes, quartered
    and blanched
1/2 pound small white mushrooms,
    quartered
1 clove garlic, minced

1 bunch asparagus, peeled, trimmed,
    blanched in boiling salted water about
    3 minutes and shocked in ice
salt and pepper to taste
4 sprigs thyme (garnish)

In a medium size saute pan, add olive oil and heat until smoking. Add potatoes and cook until golden brown (about 6 minutes). Add mushrooms and garlic and stir until mushrooms start to darken . Add asparagus tips and heat through.

Assembly

Divide the vegetable ragout between 4 heated plates. Spoon mustard sauce around vegetables and place 3 slices of pork on top.

*Beverage recommendation - Jos. Prun Wehlener Sonnenuhr Kabinett.

Doctor Bombay's Calcutta Feast

Entree

Basmati Stuffed Tomatoes with Grilled Asparagus, Yellow Squash and Portobello Mushrooms on Braised Lentil Ragout

Basmati Tomatoes

1 tablespoon olive oil
1/2 onion, diced
1 clove garlic, minced
1/2 cup basmati rice, rinsed well
1/2 teaspoon Madras curry

scant cup vegetable broth
2 green onions, sliced
2 ripe medium tomatoes, stem & core removed, halved & seedy pulp squeezed out
olive oil, salt and pepper

Preheat oven to 350° In small sauce pot add olive oil and place on medium high heat. Sweat onions and garlic (cooking without browning). When onions are translucent, add rice, curry and broth and bring to a boil. Cover and lower heat and let steam 20 minutes. Add green onions and fluff with a fork. Adjust seasoning. Cut bottom of tomato cups so they sit flush on the plate. Season insides with oil, salt and pepper and stuff with rice. Bake in covered casserole for 15 minutes. (The tomatoes can be made a day ahead and heated before serving.)

Braised Lentils

2 tablespoons olive oil
1 carrot, small dice
1 stalk celery, small dice
1/2 onion, small dice
1/2 cup lentils

1/2 teaspoon Masala Garam (available at Indian and Oriental groceries)
2 cups vegetable broth
1 teaspoon lemon juice
salt, pepper and cayenne to taste

In medium sauce pot over medium high heat, add olive oil, carrot, celery and onion and saute until lightly browned. Add lentils, Masala Garam, broth and lemon juice. Bring to a boil and then lower to simmer. Stir occasionally. Let simmer about 30 minutes or until lentils are tender but keep their shape. Adjust seasonings. Keep warm.

Grilled Asparagus, Yellow Squash and Portobello Mushrooms

(continued on page 150)

Hawaiian Macadamia Rouchers

Dessert

Delicious with vanilla ice cream.
1 3/4 cups macadamia nuts, roasted and coarsely chopped
scant 1/2 cup sugar
1 tablespoon water
1 teaspoon butter
1 1/4 cup semisweet chocolate, chopped

In small saucepan, cook sugar and water until mixture reaches soft ball stage (234°). Immediately pour nuts into syrup. Mix well and cook slowly until a light caramel color. Add butter and mix well. Pour out and cool on a cookie sheet. Melt chocolate in double boiler. Pour macadamia mixture into chocolate and mix well. Spoon the mixture into small paper or foil cups and let cool.

*Beverage recommendation - Frangelico and coffee.

Aldo Baldo
Gregory Cowan
Chef de Cuisine

Aldo Baldo was one of the first "boutique" Italian restaurants in the valley, smoothly integrating authentic food with creative twists and a fun-filled, contemporary interior. And, with many of those that followed long gone, Aldo rocks on.

Tucked in the middle of fabulous Scottsdale Fashion Square, Aldo Baldo's decor might best be described as "industrial modern." It pulses with light, bright colors and eyecatching shapes. A gleaming open kitchen offers an opportunity to watch the staff sizzle up a meal.

It is hearty, straightforward food; pastas, pizzas, grilled seafood, meat and poultry. The charm is in the inventiveness which the food is prepared. Shining examples are the polenta fritters - winner of the 1997 Scottsdale Culinary Festival Mayor's Cup, the crispy calamari salad with red potatoes and feta and prawns stuffed with goat cheese and wrapped in bacon.

New at Aldo's helm and making his presence known is Gregory Cowan. Cowan's culinary experience ranges from New York to the American South, from The Virgin Islands to a stint at The Phoenician. Cowan credits his dad for his culinary career, saying, "He was kind of a hippie earthfather, always had a garden, canned and preserved every year. He raised his own chickens and ducks and really got me tuned into food."

🐛 A kitchen tip from Greg Cowan: "When stirring rice, always use a plastic or wood utensil. Metal breaks down the grains."

Aldo Baldo: Scottsdale Fashion Square, 7014 E, Camelback Rd., Scottsdale. 994-0062
(Call for reservations and hours of business.)

Goat Cheese & Sundried Tomato Quenelles with Port Wine Glaze

Appetizer

2 tablespoons butter
2 tablespoons red onion, diced
2 cups arborio rice (available at Italian delis or specialty grocery stores such as A.J.'s)
1 cup port wine
4 cups chicken stock
2 tablespoons sundried tomatoes, julienned (not oil-packed)

1/2 cup goat cheese
1 teaspoon Italian (flat-leaved) parsley, chopped
1 cup parmesan cheese
salt and pepper to taste
1 cup semolina flour combined with 1/3 cup all purpose flour & 1 tsp fresh oregano, minced
chives (optional garnish)

Quenelles

Heat butter in saucepan over medium heat & saute onion until translucent. Add rice & stir until coated with butter. When rice starts to crackle, add port wine & continue to stir. When liquid is gone, begin to add chicken stock in 1 cup intervals, stirring until absorbed before adding more. After process is finished, allow rice to cool. Fold in goat cheese, tomatoes, parsley, parmesan and salt and pepper. Form quenelles using 2 large tablespoons. Dust in flour and oregano mixture. Fry in hot oil until golden brown.

Glaze

1 cup butter
1 small white onion, diced
1/2 cup granulated sugar

2 cups port wine
2 cups veal stock (may substitute chicken)
2 tablespoons butter

Heat butter & saute until golden. Add sugar & allow to caramelize. Add port wine & reduce by 1/3. Add veal stock & reduce again by 1/2. After reducing, strain & whisk in 2 tblsps butter.

Assembly

Spoon sauce onto 4 plates & place 2 quenelles on the sauce. Garnish with sprigs of chive.

*Beverage recommendation - Flora San Genovese.

Orange Segment and Spicy Walnut Salad

Salad

4 oranges, zested (reserve zest for garnish), peeled and segmented
1 large bulb fennel, shaved (save leaves for garnish)
1 bunch celery hearts, cut thinly on the bias (save leaves for garnish)
spicy walnuts (see recipe below)
dressing (see recipe below)

Spicy Walnuts

1 cup walnut halves
1 1/2 tablespoons brandy

2 tablespoons brown sugar
1/2 teaspoon cayenne pepper

Saute walnuts together with brown sugar. Add brandy and allow to cook until liquid evaporates. Toss nuts with cayenne pepper, spread on sheet pan and allow to cool.

Dressing

1/2 cup balsamic vinegar
1/2 cup sherry vinegar
1 teaspoon Dijon mustard

1/2 teaspoon garlic, minced
1 teaspoon Worcestershire sauce
1 teaspoon granulated sugar

Combine ingredients well in bowl or blender and allow flavors to develop.

Assembly

Toss oranges (reserving 4 segments for garnish), fennel and celery with vinaigrette to taste. Divide between 4 chilled plates, piling high and topping with spicy walnuts and reserved orange slices, fennel and celery leaves. Garnish with zest curls.

*Beverage recommendation - Sauvignon Blanc.

Tenderloin Tower with Smoked Tomato Sauce

Entree

24 ounce beef tenderloin
   cut into 8 3-ounce slices
1 large eggplant, sliced

8 1-ounce slices fresh mozzarella
1/2 cup parmesan cheese, grated
smoked tomato sauce (see recipe below)

Smoked Tomato Sauce
10 whole tomatoes, peeled
1 tablespoon olive oil
1 tablespoon onion diced

1 teaspoon garlic, minced
1/4 cup red wine
1 teaspoon fresh basil, chopped
salt and pepper to taste

Prepare barbecue. Smoke whole peeled tomatoes on the grill over wood chips. (Immerse briefly in boiling water to peel) Remove and keep grill hot for steaks and eggplant. Meanwhile, heat oil in saucepan and saute onion and garlic until golden brown. Add wine and reduce by 1/2. Add basil, seasoning and tomatoes and simmer 20 minutes.

Assembly
Preheat oven to 450° Grill beef to rare (will come to medium rare in oven). Brush eggplant with oil, season with salt & pepper & grill until soft. Build towers by stacking slices of tenderloin, eggplant, mozzarella, sauce & parmesan & then repeating to second level. Bake briefly in oven until cheese melts. Serve with red potatoes roasted with garlic, rosemary & olive oil, & sprinkled with parmesan.

*Beverage recommendation - Cabernet Sauvignon.

Lemon Dill Marinated Salmon over Angel Hair Fritatta

Entree

1/2 side Atlantic or Norwegian salmon,
   boned and skinned (about 2 pounds)
1/2 cup Dijon mustard
1 tablepoon fresh dill, chopped

1 red onion sliced thin
2 lemons, sliced thin
2 cups dry white wine
2 cups water

2 tablespoons kosher
or sea salt

Coat salmon with mustard, sprinkle with dill & spread onions & lemons down side of salmon. Lay cheese cloth over, flip salmon & spread onions & lemons on the other side. Continue wrapping with cheese cloth. Place in a large, deepish pan. Pour wine & water in pan & sprinkle with salt. Put another pan on top of fish & weight with 3 heavy cans. Refrigerate & allow salmon to cure in the brine 3 days. Then, remove from pan & thinly slice. Place slices in a pan on squares of foil.

Sauce
1 tablespoon diced shallots
1 bay leaf
2 peppercorns

2 cups white wine
1/2 cup half and half
1 tablespoon butter

1 teaspoon capers
1 teaspoon fresh dill, chopped
salt and pepper to taste

In saucepan, add shallots, bay leaf, peppercorns and wine. Reduce by 1/2. Add cream and reduce by one half again. Strain and fold in butter, capers, dill, salt and pepper.

Frittata
1/2 pound angel hair pasta
2 zucchini, peeled and julienned
1 red pepper, stemmed, seeded and julienned
3 carrots, peeled and julienned
1 yellow squash, julienned

2 eggs
1/4 cup heavy cream
salt and pepper to taste
1 red onion sliced
1 tablespoon oil

Cook the pasta in boiling, salted water until al dente, blanche, drain & cool. Blanche the vegetables (except red onion) & drain (you may use the hot pasta water). In a bowl, combine the pasta, vegetables, eggs, cream, salt & pepper. Place an omelet pan over medium heat, add olive oil & saute 1/4 of the red onion. Add one quarter pasta mixture to pan, brown on both sides. Repeat to make 4 frittatas. Quickly sear salmon in fan formations. Place a frittata on each of 4 plates & top with salmon fan & some of the sauce.

*Beverage recommendation - Pinot Grigio.

Anzio Landing

Rex Griswold
Owner

Anzio Landing is a "destination" restaurant in every sense of the word. Located virtually on the runway at Falcon Field, the restaurant is also a mini-museum dedicatedto the flying aces of World War II. Along with sweeping views of planes landing outside, the focal point of the restaurant is an actual 24 foot Cessna 402 installed over the bar.

The name of the restaurant derives from the Italian city of Anzio where the American and British forces landed in 1944. (Falcon Field, coincidentally, was built by the British in 1941 as a pilot training center.)

There is a lot more to Anzio Landing than just a clever concept and interesting and attractive ambience. Owner Rex Griswold is a graduate of Cornell School of Hotel and Restaurant Administration and he knows his Italian food. The restaurant specializes in both Northern and Southern-style dishes and is especially noted for its veal and seafood presentations.

Griswold and his wife Mary Ellen, act as restaurant hosts and have raised their three daughters to be a part of the business as well. In the little spare time the Griswolds have they are very active in the community from teaching a business class at Mesa High School for the Junior Achievement program to serving as president of the local rotary.

Cooking tip from the kitchen of Anzio Landing; "When mincing garlic, add a little salt. It pulls out the oil from the garlic, making it easier to cut."

Anzio Landing:

At the corner of Higley & McDowell (Falcon Field Airport), Mesa. 832-1188
(Call for reservations and hours of business.)

Seafood Stuffed Mushrooms

Appetizer

20 large mushroom caps
2 tablespoons butter
1/2 cup breadcrumbs
2 eggs
2 green onions, chopped
1 lb mixed seafood, cooked (crab, bay shrimp, clams and white fish)
1/4 teaspoon salt
1/4 teaspoon pepper
1 cup parmesan cheese
paprika

Preheat oven to 350° F. Melt butter in a skillet and saute mushroom caps until softened slightly. Drain on paper towel and set aside. Thoroughly combine breadcrumbs, eggs, onions, seafood and seasonings. Divide mixture evenly between mushroom caps. Bake caps about 10 minutes. Remove from oven, sprinkle with parmesan cheese and paprika. Broil about 2 minutes or until golden brown.

*Beverage recommendation - Sterling Chardonnay.

Pasta e' Fagioli

Soup (Pasta and Beans)

1/2 pound ground beef
1/2 cup onion, chopped
1/2 cup carrots, diced
1/2 cup celery, diced
1 cup fresh tomatoes, diced
32 ounces beef stock or canned broth
1 1/2 teaspoons oregano
1/2 teaspoon black pepper
1/2 teaspoon Tabasco sauce
1 cup marinara sauce (a good bottled variety is fine)
1 tablespoon parsley
1/2 cup elbow macaroni, cooked according to package directions
1 cup canned red kidney beans, drained
1 cup canned white beans, drained
parmesan cheese (optional)

Brown beef in a large saucepan. Add onions, celery, carrots and tomatoes. Cook over medium heat about 10 minutes. Add beef stock, oregano, pepper, Tabasco, marinara and parsley. Simmer for 4 hours, stirring occasionally. Just prior to serving add macaroni and beans. Sprinkle each bowl with parmesan if desired.

*Beverage Recommendation - Peroni Italian beer.

Chicken Piccatta

Entree

4 4-ounce boneless, skinless chicken breasts, pounded
flour to dredge
2 tablespoons olive oil

Sauce

1/4 cup lemon juice
1/2 tablespoon oregano
1/2 tablespoon black pepper
1 tablespoon garlic, minced
1 tablespoon chicken base or
   2 teaspoons bouillon granules

2 cups water
1/4 pound butter
1/4 cup white wine
1 tablespoon cornstarch
2 tablespoons capers, drained

In a medium saucepan, combine all sauce ingredients except wine, cornstarch and capers and bring to a boil. In a small bowl combine wine and cornstarch and add to mixture. Cook, stirring until thickened and somewhat reduced. Check and adjust seasoning. Add capers and keep warm.

Assembly

Heat 2 tablespoons olive oil in a skillet and saute floured breasts until golden brown and done through. Place on heated plates and ladle sauce over chicken breasts.

*Beverage recommendation - iced mocha cappuccino.

Veal Marsala

Entree

8 2-ounce pieces of veal cutlets, pounded out
2 tablespoons olive oil

Sauce

2 cups dry imported Italian marsala
2 cups cold water
1/2 tablespoon chicken base or 2 teaspoons bouillon granules
1 tablespoon cornstarch
1 cup mushrooms, sliced and sauteed in butter

In a heavy saucepan combine Marsala, 1 cup of water and chicken base and heat through. In a small bowl, mix the cornstarch and remaining cup of water. Stir into marsala mixture whisking until thickened and somewhat reduced. Add mushrooms and keep warm.

Assembly

In a skillet, heat olive oil and quickly sear veal. Place 2 slices veal on each of 4 heated plates and ladle with sauce.

*Beverage recommendation - Ruffino Chianti Reserva.

Armadillo Grill

Rick Gillis and
Brenda Lambrecht
Owners

Brenda Lambrecht and Rick Gillis have a combined 26 years experience in opening and operating successful restaurants in Vancouver, BC. After a trip to Phoenix, the two determined they had something to add to the valley's dining mix.

"We researched the market and saw a need for a casual neighborhood grill concept, a place that serves really good and interesting food where people can also relax and have some fun." says Lambrecht.

They found the ideal location, combining the old Pasta Segio and Azz Jazz spaces, and thus, Armadillo Grill was born. Executive chef Brett Curtis and sous chef Scott Levine, both Scottsdale Culinary Institute graduates, designed the menu to reflect the multicultural mix that is North America.

The food line-up includes such imaginative culinary interpretations as Thai chicken skewers, an Oriental quesadilla, Chesapeake crab dip and a Cajun-style seafood po' boy. And after dinner, there is a pool table available for a quick game as well as a humidor starring the Grill's signature cigars for those who enjoy a good smoke.

Armadillo Grill: 1904 E. Camelback Rd., Phoenix. 287-0700
(Call for reservations and hours of business.)

22.

Far East Avocado Dip
with Parsnip and Sweet Potato Chips

Appetizer

2 tablespoons vegetable oil
1 white onion, small dice
2 tablespoons fresh ginger, minced
2 1/2 jalapeno peppers, stemmed,
   seeded and minced

6 tablespoons cilantro, minced
small squeeze fresh lime juice
8 tablespoons tomato, small dice
salt, pepper and cumin powder to taste
3 ripe avocados, peeled seeded and mashed

Chips

2 cups parsnips, peeled and thin sliced
2 cups sweet potatoes, peeled and thin sliced
oil for frying
salt to taste

Heat oil in a saute pan and sweat onion (slowly cook but not brown) until soft.
In food processor combine onion, ginger, jalapeno, cilantro and lime and pulse
until minced together. Do not overprocess. Place avocado meat in a bowl, add
vegetable and seasoning mix and mash together to make a smooth paste.
Cover and refrigerate while preparing chips. Heat oil in deep fryer or pan and
fry unti crisp and golden. Season to taste and serve with dip.

*Beverage recommendation - Honey Wheat Ale.

Penne Arrabiata

Entree

4 6-ounce boneless, skinless chicken breasts
2 red bell peppers cut in 1/2 inch strips
1 1/2 teaspoons cayenne pepper
1 1/2 pounds penne pasta
2 teaspoons olive oil
1 tablespoon fresh garlic, minced
4 tablespoons minced shallot (or, any other onion)

2 cups white wine
1 cup sundried tomatoes, julienned
1/2 cup prepared pesto sauce
2 cups heavy cream
1/2 cup parmesan cheese
salt and pepper to taste
basil leaves for garnish (optional)

Preheat broiler. Place chicken breasts on broiler pan and red pepper strips on a
baking sheet. Sprinkle peppers with cayenne. Broil chicken until golden brown
and done and peppers until they are fork tender (about 20 minutes). Set aside. At
this point begin cooking pasta in boiling salted water until al dente. In a saucepan,
heat olive oil and saute garlic and onion . Deglaze pan with white wine and reduce
the liquid, adding the tomatoes and cooking about 2 -3 minutes. Then add pesto,
cream and seasonings and stir until fully incorporated. Add drained pasta to sauce
and toss. Divide pasta mixture between 4 warm plates. Top each with a chicken
breast, red peppers, parmesan and basil leaves.

*Beverage recommendation - Bloody Mary made with lemon vodka.

Tomato Towers
with Yogurt Cucumber Mint Sauce

Salad

12 large roma tomatoes, tops cut off
    and hollowed out
8 canned artichokes, drained and minced
1/2 cup feta cheese, crumbled
1/2 cup fresh basil, cut in narrow strips

1/2 cup white onion, small dice
1/2 cup yellow bell pepper, small dice
1/2 cup black olives, small dice
8 teaspoons garlic, minced
salt and pepper to taste

Combine all ingredients except tomatoes and refrigerate for one hour.

Yogurt Cucumber Mint Sauce

2 cups plain yogurt
1 1/2 cucumbers, skinned, seeded and diced
3 cloves garlic, minced
1/2 cup mint leaves, minced

8 tablespoons olive oil
4 tablespoons red onion, fine dice
1/2 cup fresh lemon juice
sugar, salt and white pepper to taste

Strain water out of yogurt by placing it in cheesecloth and hanging over sink for an hour (tieing it to the faucet works well). Combine rest of ingredients with yogurt and refrigerate for 1 hour.

Stuff tomatoes with vegetable mix until it is mounded over top. Spoon yogurt sauce on each of 4 chilled plates. Arrange tomatoes in a triangle and if desired, garnish with sprouts, green onion and a carrot brush.

*Beverage recommendation - Cabernet or Merlot.

Maylasian Shrimp

Entree

20 16/20 size shrimp, peeled with
    tail left on and butterflied
1 tablespoon butter
1 cup red pepper, julienned
1 cup yellow bell pepper, julienned
1/2 cup carrots, julienned
1/2 cup celery, julienned
2 red onions, cut in thin strips
1 cup pineapple juice

3 cups coconut milk (available at
    Oriental groceries and Cost Plus)
2 teaspoons cumin
4 teaspoons red chile powder
2 teaspoons tumeric
4 cups short grain white rice
1/2 cup cold butter
salt and pepper to taste

In heavy skillet, heat butter and saute the vegetables until fork tender. Add the pineapple juice and coconut milk and bring to a medium simmer. Add the seasonings and then the shrimp. Poach until shrimp firm up and turn pink (don't overcook). Remove vegetables and shrimp from pan and reduce liquid until syrupy. In another pan, prepare rice according to package directions. Divide rice, shrimp and veggies between 4 heated plates. Take the reduction liquid off the heat and stir in butter until incorporated. Ladle around the rice.

*Beverage recommendation - Mai Tais.

Baby Kay's
Cajun Kitchen
Baby Kay Romero
Owner

"I'm no chef, cher," tiny, blond Baby Kay insists in her inimitable Cajun accent, "just a damn good cook." And that has been more than enough for the multitudes who've been trooping to her restaurants since the first one opened 9 years ago.

There's nothing that's not colorful about the lady. She was born in Rochelle, Lousiana, a town that is no longer there. The courthouse and all its records burned, so Baby Kay calls herself a misplaced coonass. On the bright side, she says, nobody knows how old she is.

She credits her cooking skills to her mother-in-law. When Kay married husband Rosie, she couldn't even boil water. Rosie's mom thought her son was doomed and took the young bride in hand.

When she, Rosie and their 8 kids got settled in Phoenix, it soon became apparent there was a serious absence of Cajun cooking to be found. (According to Kay, "You don't throw shrimp, chicken, beans, cayenne and whatnot in a pot and call it Cajun!") So at the urging of family and friends Kay decided to open a very small restaurant. The rest has been Valley culinary history as the Romeros's continue to cook up a storm and "Lessez Le Bon Ton Rouler" (let the good times roll).

🐚 A tip from Baby Kay's kitchen: "Assemble all ingredients in the recipe & then combine with fun companions, good music & your favorite beverage."

Baby Kay's: 7216 E. Shoeman Lane, Scottsdale. 990-9080.
2119 E. Camelback Rd. (Town and Country Village), Phoenix.
955-0011
(Call for reservations and hours of business.)

Shrimp Remoulade

Appetizer

There are several versions of remoulade sauce. The original contains no mayonnaise. In many places the sauce is red but Baby Kay prefers it white.

16 jumbo shrimp, peeled, deveined, boiled and chilled

Sauce
1 cup mayonnaise
juice of one lemon
5 cloves garlic, minced
1 tablespoon Creole mustard (such as Zatarain's)
1/2 cup fresh horseradish, grated
Tabasco to taste
1/2 cup fresh parsley
salt to taste

Combine all ingredients and chill. Serve over cold shrimp.

*Beverage recommendation - Sauvignon Blanc.

Lagniappe Salad with Blue Cheese Dressing

Salad

Lagniappe means "that little extra something."

1 cup each red leaf lettuce, green leaf lettuce and spinach
1 small red onion, thinly sliced
1/2 cup purple cabbage, shredded
4 hard boiled eggs, sliced
1/2 cup bacon, crisp-fried bacon and crumbled
1/2 cup andouille sausage, fried (available at Schreiner's Sausage)
1 cup white cheddar cheese, cubed
1 cup croutons

Dressing
1/2 cup mayonnaise
1/4 cup sour cream
1 cup blue cheese, crumbled
Louisiana hot sauce to taste
salt and pepper to taste

Combine all ingredients well.

In a large salad bowl, toss lettuce and spinach together. Distribute the onion and cabbage on top. Divide bowl into 4 sections, fill 1/4 with hard-boiled egg, 1/4 with bacon, 1/4 with cheese and 1/4 with sausage. Pool dressing in center. Don't toss.

*Beverage recommendation - Pinot Noir.

Jambalaya

Entree

A unique Cajun dish that resembles a rice dressing.

1 tablespoon vegetable oil
1 pound chicken thigh meat, boneless, skinless and cut into chunks
1 pound andouille sausage (available at Schreiner's Sausage) or other good smoked sausage, cut in chunks
1 cup onions, chopped
1/2 cup green bell peppers, chopped
1/2 cup celery, chopped
1 1/4 cups long grain white rice (not instant)
2 1/2 cups chicken broth
salt, pepper and cayenne to taste
chopped green onion for garnish

In medium dutch oven brown chicken. Add sausage. Stir and cook 5 minutes. Add "Cajun Holy Trinity" (onions, bell peppers and celery) and stir well until onions wilt, about 5 minutes. Add rice and broth. Bring to a boil. Cover and reduce heat to low. Stir every 10 minutes until rice is done (about 25 minutes). Serve with green onions.

*Beverage recommendation - Ice Cold Beer.

Barbecued Shrimp

Entree

This is not your traditional barbecue. Instead the shrimp are baked in a spicy butter sauce.

24 jumbo shrimp, peeled and deveined
2 cups prepared rice

Sauce
2 sticks butter
1 large lemon, thinly sliced
1 cup Worcestershire sauce
black pepper and cayenne to taste (Cajuns like it spicy, cher!)

Preheat oven to 300° In a saucepan over medium heat, melt butter. Add lemon, Worcestershire and seasonings and bring to a boil. Place shrimp in a baking dish, pour butter over and bake until just turning pink and the tails curl. Arrange shrimp in a circular pattern on a heated platter with rice in the center and pour sauce over all. Serve with crusty French bread to sop up sauce.

*Beverage recommendation - Chardonnay.

Bill Johnson's
Big Apple Restaurant
Johnny Johnson
Owner

In the forty plus years since The Big Apple opened on East Van Buren, generations of Phoenix families have trooped through the doors. And, they keep on a'comin' because no place else in town has quite the same combination of rustic Western charm, friendly staff and hearty, down-home food at reasonable prices.

Founded by Bill and Gene Johnson, the restaurant originally doubled as a radio broadcast center with Bill hosting a nightly variety show. Among the guests over the years were such luminaries as Waylon Jennings, Rex Allen, Jim Reeves, Buck Owens and Tex Ritter. After Johnson died, his son Johnny kept the show going until 1972.

Entertainment aside (and that includes the eye-filling Old West decor), the big draw of The Big Apple has always been the food which stars succulent barbecue meats and chicken, country breakfasts, and the house specialty, a gut-bustin' 28 ounce Porterhouse steak. Their famous deep-dish apple pie is made from Mrs. Gene Johnson's original recipe.

Still family owned and operated, Bill Johnson's Big Apple has expanded to a booming mini-chain of five restaurants.

Bill Johnson's Big Apple Restaurant:
3757 E. Van Buren St., Phoenix. 275-2107
3101 W. Indian School Rd., Phoenix. 277-6291
16810 N. 19th Ave., Phoenix. 863-7921
950 E. Main St., Mesa. 969-6504
3110 N. Arizona Ave., Chandler. 892-2542

Barbecued Shrimp

Appetizer

16 large shrimp, peeled and deveined
8 mushroom caps
8 cubes pineapple
4 cherry tomatoes
Bill Johnson's Regular Barbecue Sauce (available at most local grocery stores)

Soak 4 5-inch skewers in water about 15 minutes. Thread each skewer alternately with 4 shrimp, 2 mushrooms, 2 cubes pineapple and 1 cherry tomato. Place under broiler or on grill and baste with sauce. Cook 5 minutes or until shrimp are pink and firm and vegetables soften.
Serve with extra sauce.

*Beverage recommendation - Margaritas.

Western Chili

Entree

Any leftover chili can be frozen.

4 pounds beef, coarsely ground
1 onion, finely chopped
1 bell pepper, finely chopped
1/4 cup tomato puree
1 1/2 teaspoon black pepper
1 teaspoon garlic powder
2 teaspoons salt
1/2 teaspoon cayenne pepper
1/2 teaspoon thyme
1/2 teaspoon oregano
4 tablespoons pure chili powder
1 tablespoon Albuquerque red chili pepper
1 teaspoon red chiles, crushed
1 16 ounce can whole peeled tomatoes
2 tablespoons all purpose flour
1/2 pound dried pinto beans, precooked (or substitute 2 16-ounce cans of pintos which have been drained)

Cook beef, onions and bell peppers in a large saucepan until meat is well-browned and vegetables have softened. Add the next 13 ingredients. Mix thoroughly and cook 20 minutes. Strain off grease. In a small saucepan blend together 4 tablespoons of the grease and the flour over medium heat until it makes a thick roux. Add the roux back into the chili stirring constantly until chili thickens. Add pinto beans and simmer 1 - 1 1/2 hours.

Barbecued Ribs

Entree

4 pounds beef or pork ribs cut into serving sized pieces
1 large onion, sliced
1 bay leaf
2 cloves
1 teaspoon salt
1 18 ounce bottle Bill Johnson's Regular or Hickory Barbecue Sauce

Place ribs in a large kettle and cover with water. Add onion, bay leaf, cloves and salt and heat to boiling. Reduce heat, cover and simmer 1 to 1 1/2 hours or until meat is tender. Remove ribs from water. Brush each side generously with barbecue sauce. Place ribs in a pyrex baking dish and cover with foil. Do not allow foil to touch meat. Refrigerate 2 hours or overnight. Grill meat 6 inches from the coals, turning and basting frequently with remaining sauce. Cook a total of 15 - 20 minutes or until nicely browned.

* Beverage recommendation for the ribs and chili — cold beer.

Banana Cake

Dessert

Johnny says this recipe was one made by his great grandmother. When the bananas are placed between the cake layers, the entire cake absorbs the flavor. Use a yellow cake mix if you don't have time to make it from scratch.

3 cups cake flour, sifted
3 1/2 teaspoons baking powder
1/2 teaspoon salt
2/3 cup butter or margarine
1 3/4 cup sugar

2 eggs
1 1/2 teaspoon vanilla
1 1/4 cup milk
2 bananas, thinly sliced

Frosting
1/2 cup butter or margarine
1/4 cup milk
1 teaspoon vanilla
4 cups powdered sugar

Preheat oven to 350 F. Grease and flour 2 8-inch round cake pans, Sift together flour, baking powder and salt. In another bowl, cream butter or margarine and sugar until fluffy. Add eggs and vanilla and beat until completely mixed. Add flour mixture to creamed mixture, alternating with milk. Beat well after each addition. Pour into prepared pans. Bake for 30 - 35 minutes or until toothpick inserted in the center comes out clean. Let cool 10 minutes in the pans and then turn out on a rack. When cakes are completely cool, frost one layer with vanilla frosting. Arrange sliced bananas on first layer. Top with second layer and frost top and sides.

* Beverage recommendation — hot coffee or iced tea.

Bistro 24

The Ritz-Carlton, Phoenix
Anthony Keene
Executive Chef

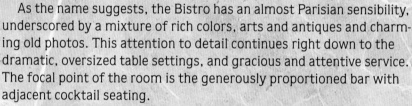

The opening of Bistro 24 has turned the 24th Street and Camelback area on its metaphorical ear. Suddenly, this is the most sought after restaurant in a neighborhood that includes some of the Valley's best.

As the name suggests, the Bistro has an almost Parisian sensibility, underscored by a mixture of rich colors, arts and antiques and charming old photos. This attention to detail continues right down to the dramatic, oversized table settings, and gracious and attentive service. The focal point of the room is the generously proportioned bar with adjacent cocktail seating.

Chef Anthony Keene oversees all three meals served at the restaurant and has designed the fare to be a contemporary reading of traditional bistro cuisine. There is an intelligent wine list to match. Dishes such as duck hash star at breakfast and of course, there is tuna nicoise at lunch. Dinner features an outstanding seafood risotto as well as the classic steak au poivre with frites.

With an extensive background in French cuisine as well as twelve years with the Ritz organization, Keene fits perfectly in the environment. Even his off-duty pursuits are linked, he is an avid home gardener specializing in herbs and produce.

Bistro 24: The Ritz-Carlton, Phoenix, 2401 E. Camelback Rd., Phoenix. 952-2424
(Call for reservations and hours of business.)

Pea and Curry Soup

Soup

Frozen peas will also give great results. Select a mild curry that won't over-power the sweetness of the peas.

4 tablespoons olive oil
1 pound fresh English peas, cooked
1/2 yellow onion, chopped
2 celery ribs, chopped

2 tablespoons curry
2 quarts chicken stock
1 head Boston lettuce, chopped
salt and pepper to taste

Heat oil in a stockpot and add peas, onions and celery. Saute the vegetables. Do not brown. Add lettuce and curry and continue to cook 2 additional minutes. Add stock and simmer 15 - 20 minutes. Place soup in blender and puree until smooth. Season with salt and pepper and serve immediately.

*Beverage recommendation - King Estate, Pinot Gris.

Baked Goat Cheese, Watercress and Belgian Endive Salad with Walnut Vinaigrette

Salad

1 pound goat cheese
3 eggs

2 tablespoons walnut oil
salt and pepper to taste

Preheat oven to 350°. Place goat cheese in a mixer and process until smooth. Add eggs, oil and salt and pepper and continue blending until eggs are incorpo-rated. Divide mixture between 4 2 ounce ovenproof cups and bake in water bath for 20 minutes or until firm. Set aside.

1 bunch watercress, cleaned and torn
2 heads Belgian endive, cleaned and divided into leaves
1 head butter lettuce, cleaned and divided into leaves
1/2 red onion, julienned
20 carmelized walnuts (sprinkle with about 2 tablespoons sugar and bake in 350° oven until sugar has melted and nuts have browned)
2 tomatoes, peeled, seeded and finely diced
vinaigrette (see recipe below)

Vinaigrette

3 tablespoons Dijon mustard
1 tablespoon red wine vinegar

1 cup walnut oil
salt and pepper to taste

Combine all ingredients and set aside.

Assembly

Place watercress, lettuce, red onion, walnuts and tomato in a bowl and toss. Add vinaigrette, retoss and divide between 4 chilled plates. Top each salad with goat cheese timbale and serve.

*Beverage recommendation - Chateau Saint Michelle, Columbia Valley.

Grilled Lamb Saddle

Entree

For autumn dining, substitute mushrooms and squash for the artichoke and zucchini. Leftovers make an excellent sandwich with red onion marmalade on pita bread.

1 whole boned and cleaned lamb saddle
1 clove garlic, minced
1 bunch rosemary, chopped (save 4 sprigs for garnish)
1/4 tablespoon black pepper, fresh cracked

Marinade

1/2 bottle red zinfandel
1 bunch thyme
1 cup Dijon mustard

1/2 onion, sliced
1 quart vegetable oil
1 cup extra virgin olive oil

Combine all ingredients.

(continued on page 150)

Chicken Fricassee with Potato Gnocchi

Entree

The gnocchi in this recipe makes a great appetizer on their own.

4 8-ounce boneless, skinless chicken breasts cut in strips
4 tablespoons olive oil
1/4 cup of dry white wine
1 cup chicken stock
1 cup heavy cream
1 tablespoon each fresh basil, sage, tarragon and spinach, finely chopped
24 gnocchi (see recipe below)
1/4 cup tomato, peeled, seeded and diced

Place skillet on medium heat, add oil. When oil is hot, add chicken strips to pan a few at a time. Cook chicken until lightly browned. Deglaze pan with wine and reduce by half. Add stock and cream and reduce by half again. Add herbs, salt and pepper. Set aside and keep warm.

Gnocchi

5 pounds russet potatoes, baked with skin on
6 egg yolks
4 cups all purpose flour
1 tablespoon Kosher or sea salt

2 teaspoons nutmeg,
   fresh grated if possible
1/4 cup all purpose flour

When potatoes cool, skin and press flesh through a fine sieve into a bowl. Add egg yolks and mix thoroughly. In a separate bowl. mix 4 cups flour with the salt and nutmeg. Add the flour mixture to the warm potato puree and mix by hand until all flour is incorporated. Let dough rest about 1/2 hour. Sprinkle work surface with flour and roll out to 1 inch thickness. Cut to desired shape. Cook gnocchi in rapidly boiling, salted water for 3 - 5 minutes (they float to the top when cooked). Drain carefully.

Assembly

Place chicken on warm serving platter with gnocchi. If desired, serve with steamed asparagus, English peas and portobello mushrooms. Garnish with chopped tomato and serve immediately.

*Beverage recommendation - Sonoma-Cutrer Russian River Ranches Chardonnay, Sonoma.

Cafe Patou
Philippe Forcioli
Chef-Owner

One could almost say Philippe Forcioli was destined to cook. Born in Southern France, his grandmother was for years chef at the French president's summer residence. In addition, his mother was an accomplished home cook. So, it was no great stretch that Forcioli decided to attend culinary school.

After graduation, his first job was as a chef on a French cruise line. Travel quickly became as vital to Forcioli as wielding a whisk, and he eventually was employed by the fabled Orient Express. When the Orient Express Company bought The Lodge at Vail in Colorado, he moved there. After a stint in New York with Harry Cipriani, Forcioli and his wife Anna, moved to her hometown of Rockford, Illinois and there, Cafe Patou debuted.

The Scottsdale branch of Cafe Patou has thrilled diners eager for a taste of food with an International flair. French is definitely the restaurant's culinary language of choice (it is also echoed in the very Gallic decor), but there are also influences that range from Thai and Caribbean to that of the American West. All, of course, are a reflection of Forcioli's travels.

Though a relative newcomer to town, the Cafe is already famous for toothsome flatbreads with various imaginative toppings, sumptuous desserts and delicate but full-flavored crepes.

Cafe Patou: 7000 E. Shea Blvd. (Scottsdale Promenade), Scottsdale. 951-6868
(Call for reservations and hours of business.)

Appetizers

With a salad and dessert these crepes also make a satisfying entree.

Crepes

7 ounces butter	1 quart milk
14 ounces flour	2 pinches salt
6 whole eggs	3 1/2 ounces sugar

Melt the butter. Put flour in a mixing bowl making a well in the center. Crack eggs into the middle. Sprinkle salt and sugar around flour. Incorporate milk slowly. Strain through a fine sieve, Incorporate the melted butter. Place in refrigerator for at least 2 hours. Make crepes in a non-stick pan with a half teaspoon of butter for the first crepe. You don't need to add any butter after the first one. Make the crepes as thin as possible, cooking about 30 seconds on each side. This recipe will make about 40 crepes depending on the size of pan you use. Extra batter will keep in the refrigerator. Leftover crepes can be frozen.

Ratatouille and Goat Cheese Filling

1 cup extra virgin olive oil	1 teaspoon fresh garlic, diced
2 cups yellow squash, diced	1 tablespoon salt
2 cups zucchini, diced	1 teaspoon pepper
2 cups eggplant, diced	1/2 cup fresh basil, julienned
1 cup red peppers, diced	2 cups goat cheese
1 cup onions, diced	8 crepes
4 cups fresh tomatoes, diced	2 cups parmesan cheese, grated

Heat olive oil in a skillet and saute vegetables in order listed. Add salt and pepper. Let simmer 12 minutes. Add basil. Add chunks of goat cheese stirring gently. Divide filling among 8 crepes, sprinkle with parmesan and place under broiler 30 seconds or until slightly golden.

Chicken Breast Filling

2 tablespoons olive oil
2 boneless, skinless chicken breasts, diced in 1/2 inch cubes
(Philippe recommends using free range chicken)
1/2 teaspoon fresh garlic, chopped
2 tablespoons whole grain mustard
4 cups mushrooms, sliced and sauteed
salt and pepper to taste
3 cups heavy cream
3 cups veal or beef demi-glace
1 tablespoon chives, chopped
4 large or 8 small crepes
4 cups Swiss cheese, grated

Preheat broiler. Put skillet on high heat. When pan is hot add olive oil and chicken, Do not stir chicken, let it brown on just one side. Add garlic, mustard, cooked mushrooms, salt and pepper. Stir just enough to cook garlic, Add the cream, demi-glace and chives, Stir and reduce for 2 minutes. Taste for seasonings and consistency. Divide filling among crepes. Sprinkle with Swiss cheese and broil until cheese is melted.

*Beverage recommendations - With the Ratatouille Crepes, Meridian Chardonnay. With the Chicken Crepes, a Beaujolais or Petite Sirah.

Red Snapper en Papillotte

Entree

4 whole red snappers with heads on, 1-1/2 pounds dressed and scaled
4 cloves garlic
4 bay leaves
4 sprigs thyme
4 sprigs rosemary
2 cups carrots, julienned
2 cups onions, diced
3 cups dry white wine
salt and pepper to taste
4 slices lemon
4 pieces baking parchment or aluminum foil large enough to wrap fish completely

Sauce

1 teaspoon olive oil
2 cloves garlic, chopped
4 cups fresh tomato, diced
1/2 cup water
6 leaves basil, julienned
salt and pepper to taste

Heat olive oil in a skillet and sautee garlic until golden. Add tomatoes, water, basil, salt and pepper and cook through.

Preheat oven to 400° Place garlic, bay leaves, thyme and rosemary inside fish. Season inside and out with salt and pepper. Place on aluminum foil. Distribute carrots, onions and white wine over each. Place lemon slice on each fish and wrap well. Bake 30 minutes. Serve fish in the foil with sauce on side.

*Beverage recommendation - Muscadet.

Salmon au jus de Carotte

Entree

8 6-ounce salmon filets
4 cups carrot juice
1 teaspoon lemon juice
pinch cayenne pepper
1 tablespoon lemongrass, chopped (available at gourmet and Oriental grocery stores)
4 leaves basil, julienned
salt to taste

Steam, poach or grill salmon until firm and opaque but not overcooked. Warm carrot juice together with all other ingredients, do not boil. Plate salmon filets and ladle with sauce.

*Beverage recommendation - Gewurztraminer.

Cajun House
Dustin Booth
Executive Chef

Cajun House is the metaphorical new kid on the block, and a brawny youngster it is. Covering 25,000 feet, it includes not only a restaurant but concert space, a piano bar, an oyster bar and a gift shop.

The enormous interior has been designed to replicate one of the historic streets of New Orleans French Quarter from the lacy wrought iron balconies overhead right down to the cobbled street underfoot.

An evening at Cajun House is a complete experience starting with dinner in The Jazz Room, which features such regional specialties as blackened red snapper, fried alligator tenderloin and bananas Foster. Afterwards, guests can play pool, enjoy live music or just relax and sip an authentic Hurricane.

Chef Dustin Booth has blazed his way through some of the Valley's finest kitchen's. As executive chef of Cajun House, Booth plans to creatively integrate Southwestern influences into the restaurant's Cajun-Creole cuisine.

❦ Kitchen Tip From Chef Booth: When using a roux to thicken or flavor a dish, try experimenting. The darker the roux, the more flavor it will impart. Try adding spices and vegetables to the roux to give it a different flair. The three most common rouxs are blonde, brown and black depending on how long they are cooked. Remember, the darker the roux, the less it will thicken.

Cajun House: 7117 E. Third Ave., Scottsdale. 945-5150 (Call for reservations and hours of business.)

Red Beans and Rice

Appetizer

1 lb dried red kidney beans
2 cups Cajun Holy Trinity (equal parts chopped celery, bell pepper & onion)
1/4 pound butter
1 cup dark brown sugar
6 bay leaves
large hambone or two ham hocks

1/4 cup Cajun seasoning
6 tablespoons Tabasco
1 1/2 gallon water
4 Andouille sausages (available at Schreiner's Sausage, or two large smoked sausages)
2 cups cooked rice
1 bunch green onions, chopped

Sort beans for rocks and rinse. Melt butter in a large stockpot, saute beans and Holy Trinity. Add next 5 ingredients and water. Bring to a boil. Reduce heat to medium high and cook about one hour, stirring frequently. Add more water if necessary. The beans should be completely soft and the overall consistency semi-thick, almost like a gravy. Remove hambone or hocks, cut off meat and return to pot. Split sausage links lengthwise and brown in a skillet. Spoon rice into bowls and cover with beans. Place links on top and sprinkle with green onions.

*Beverage recommendation - Blackened Voodoo Lager.

Seafood Gumbo

Soup

2 cups Cajun Holy Trinity (equal parts celery, onion and bell pepper)
4 cloves garlic, chopped
2 tablespoons parsley, chopped
1/2 cup Cajun seasoning
1 gallon water
1 cup clam juice
1/2 cup Tabasco sauce

3 tablespoons gumbo file (available in the spice section of most supermarkets)
2 cups black roux (see recipe below)
1 pound frozen okra, cut in 1/4 inch pieces
1 pound rock shrimp
4 blue crabs, shell on and split
1 cup cooked rice

Roux

1 pound butter
2 cups flour

1 cup Cajun Holy Trinity
1/2 cup Cajun seasoning

Melt butter in saucepan. Add flour slowly. Cook on medium heat, constantly whisking roux until it becomes a dark brown color. Add Trinity and seasoning. Continue to cook until roux is very dark. (It is important not to burn the roux, so use your nose!)

Assembly

In a large saucepan saute Holy Trinity, garlic and parsley in butter with Cajun seasoning. When onions become transparent, add water. Stir in clam juice and bring to a boil. Add Gumbo file, Tabasco and roux. Whisk thoroughly until roux is completely dissolved. Bring soup to a boil and add okra, crabs and shrimp. Continue to cook over medium high heat for approximately 5 minutes. Ladle soup into bowl, placing crab claw over edge of bowl so it looks like it is trying to crawl out. Top with 1/4 cup rice.

*Beverage recommendation - Puligny Montrachet.

Coq au Vin

Entree

This serves more than 4 but assures that each person gets the type of meat they prefer and, the leftovers are yummy.

2 chickens, quartered (about 3 lbs apiece)
1 cup red wine vinegar
1/2 cup dark brown sugar

Place a large saute pan on the stove and heat on high for 2 minutes, Marinate the chicken in brown sugar and vinegar while pan is heating. You don't want too much of the vinegar flavor to penetrate the chicken. Place chicken in pan skin side down and cook until skin is golden brown. Turn & repeat. Remove chicken from pan & reserve.

2 tablespoons butter
1/2 cup onion, chopped
1/2 cup bell pepper, chopped
1/4 cup celery, chopped
1/4 cup garlic, chopped
1/4 cup carrot, chopped
2 cups red wine

1/2 gallon water
1 cup brown sugar
1/4 cup Tabasco sauce
1/2 cup mushrooms (preferably shiitake, morels, portobello, etc.)
1 tablespoon blond roux
browned chicken quarters

In a large stockpot heat butter, and saute onions, peppers, celery, garlic and carrots. When vegetables have softened, add red wine. Reduce by half. Add water, sugar, Tabasco and chicken quarters. Bring to a boil and cook 20 minutes or until chicken begins to separate from the bone. Remove chicken from liquid. Continue to reduce liquid about 20 minutes. Place chicken back in the pot with mushrooms, return to a boil and add roux. Stir thoroughly. When sauce is thick remove the chicken. Place two quarters chicken on each plate and spoon sauce over.

*Beverage recommendation - Louis Latour Chateau Corton Grancey.

Shrimp Creole

Entree

20 large shrimp, peeled and deveined
1 cup vegetable oil
2 tablespoons flour
2 tablespoons butter

2 tablespoons green onions, chopped
2 cups cooked rice, kept warm
Creole sauce (see recipe below)

Heat oil in large saute pan. Dust shrimp with flour, knocking off excess. Place in oil and cook until shrimp turn pink and become firm. Remove and drain on absorbent paper or cloth. Melt butter in another pan, when it is almost liquefied add onions and cook until hot through. Set butter aside.

Creole Sauce

10 ripe tomatoes, quartered
1/2 cup garlic, sliced
1 cup worcestershire sauce
2 bay leaves
1 2 tablespoons fresh thyme, chopped
4 tablespoons fresh oregano, chopped

2 tablespoons Tabasco sauce
2 teaspoons cayenne pepper
1/3 cup yellow onion, chopped
1/3 cup green bell pepper, chopped
1/4 cup celery, chopped
1/4 cup parsley, chopped

(continued on page 150)

Camelback Inn
Marriott
Gary Scherer
Executive Chef

In all the world, only one - that's how Camelback Inn has been described since it opened sixty years ago in the desert outside of Phoenix. Situated at the base of Mummy Mountain on 125 acres, the rustic yet elegant resort has received the coveted Mobil Five Star Award for 28 consecutive years and the AAA Five Diamond Award for 24 years.

It is no wonder, given the beautiful accommodations and incredible amenities that include oasis-like pools, lighted tennis courts, a European-style spa, seven restaurants and lounges throughout the property as well as access to two 18 hole championship golf courses.

The Chaparral restaurant is world-famous for its impeccable Continental cuisine. The Southwestern-accented Navajo serves breakfast lunch and dinner while Sprouts restaurant at The Spa is well regarded for food that is as flavorful as it is healthy.

All food service is under the direction of Gary Scherer who heads up a staff of over 100 people. European-born and trained Patrick Peeters is Camelback Inn's pastry chef and is in charge of the bake shop which prepares all the bread, rolls and delectable desserts served in the resort. Graduates of the prestigious Culinary Institute of American are prevalent at Camelback Inn with David Schneider heading up the Navajo, Mark Henry in the Chaparral and Steve Haughie chef at Sprouts.

Camelback Inn: 5402 E. Lincoln Dr., Scottsdale. 948-1700
(Call for reservations and hours of business.)

The Chaparral's World Famous Lobster Bisque

Soup

1 cup of lobster meat, reserved	1 cup brandy
3 pounds fresh lobster bodies	1 tablespoon sherry
1 medium onion, roughly chopped	1 teaspoon cracked red pepper
1 stalk celery, roughly chopped	1 teaspoon cracked black pepper
1 carrot, roughly chopped	1 cup heavy cream
1/2 leek, roughly chopped	2 - 3 tablespoons butter
2 cloves garlic	salt and pepper to taste
1/2 cup olive oil	1 sheet puff pastry
1/2 bunch tarragon, chopped	flour
1/4 cup tomato paste	1 egg, whisked

Preheat oven to 400°. Split lobster shells in half. Remove roe and tomalley and reserve. Crush shells and toss with onion, celery, carrot, leek, garlic and olive oil. Add tarragon and toss again. Spread on a baking sheet and roast 30 minutes (after 15 minutes, spread tomato paste on shells and continue baking). When shells are bright red, remove from oven and saute in a hot pan for 3 minutes. Add brandy and flame. Saute for another minute. Transfer shells and vegetables to a large stockpot and cover with water. Bring to a boil, reduce heat and simmer for 45 minutes. Remove from heat and strain liquid. Return liquid to the pot and bring to a simmer. Skim off fat with a ladle and transfer to another pan. Add flour to reserved fat, and whisk, making a roux. Add roux to strained liquid and simmer 10 to 15 minutes. Add sherry, peppers, cream, butter, salt and pepper. Ladle bisque into 4 ovenproof ceramic bowls and divide reserved lobster meat between the bowls. Lay a sheet of puff pastry on a floured surface and cut 4 circles large enough to fit over top of bowls. Brush egg over one side of each pastry circle, lightly scoring the same side (don't cut all the way through). Place pastry circles over top of bowls pinching edges to seal. Place bowls in 400° oven until pastry has risen and is golden brown and flaky.

*Beverage recommendation - champagne.

Sprouts' Sedona Sunset Shrimp and Lemon Pepper Pasta

Entree

12 large shrimp	1 cup spiced dark rum
12 ounces lemon pepper pasta, cooked al dente and drained	4 tablespoons roasted garlic
	1 cup vegetable stock
1 tablespoon olive oil	2 tablespoons cilantro, chopped
1/2 red onion, large dice	juice of 1 lime
1 cup red, green and yellow peppers, large dice	salt to taste
	2 thinly sliced scallions (garnish)

In a large skillet over medium high heat, lightly saute onions and peppers in olive oil. Add shrimp and cook about a minute on each side. Remove pan from heat and add rum. Return pan to stove so rum burns off. Add the roasted garlic, vegetable stock, lime juice, cilantro and pasta. Mix well and cook 2 minutes or until pasta is hot. Place pasta in a serving bowl and garnish with green onions.

*Beverage recommendation - Chardonnay.

Pan Seared Pistachio Crusted Halibut
with Strawberry Chile Compote a la Navajo

Entree

8 3-ounce pieces halibut
2 tablespoons olive oil
1 tablespoon ground ginger, dry roasted
fresh ground pepper and kosher
   or sea salt to taste

1/2 cup pistachio nuts, shelled and ground
1/2 cup all purpose flour
4 tablespoons olive oil
strawberry chile compote (see recipe below)

Strawberry Chile Compote

1 pint strawberries, washed, stemmed and cut into 1/4's or 1/6's depending on size
1/2 anaheim chile, stemmed and seeded, diced
1/4 red onion, diced
1/2 yellow bell pepper, diced
1/2 daikon radish, diced (about 1/2 cup, jicama may be substituted)
1/2 cup strained strawberry jam
1 tablespoon Chambord (raspberry liqueur)
1 tablespoon brown sugar
fresh ground pepper and kosher or sea salt to taste

In a bowl combine all ingredients and season to taste. Set aside.

Assembly

Combine olive oil and ginger in bowl and marinate halibut for 1 hour. Combine pistachios and flour making sure it is well-blended. Dredge halibut pieces in mixture. Heat olive oil in skillet and pan fry halibut over medium heat until golden brown on all sides and fish is desired doneness. Place two pieces fish and several spoonfuls of compote on each plate.

*Beverage recommendation - Vouvray.

Holiday Gingerbread House

Dessert

This is a visual dessert, which can be used as a centerpiece, as well as an edible one. The house can be decorated according to the season - in orange and black for Halloween and Thanksgiving, red and green for Christmas, pastels for Easter, etc.

sturdy cardboard for the base
paper patterns for walls, roof, chimney, etc.
gingerbread (see recipe below)
royal icing (see recipe below)
food coloring (optional)
assorted candies for decorating such as peppermints, gumdrops, M&M's, etc.

Gingerbread

1 1/4-pound unsalted butter
1 1/4-pound granulated sugar
3 eggs
2 pints molasses
2 tablespoons cider vinegar
5 pounds all purpose flour

1 teaspoon baking soda
1 teaspoon salt
2 teaspoons ground ginger
3 teaspoons ground cinnamon
pinch of ground cloves
pinch of nutmeg

(continued on page 151)

Capers
Larry Marcus
Executive Chef

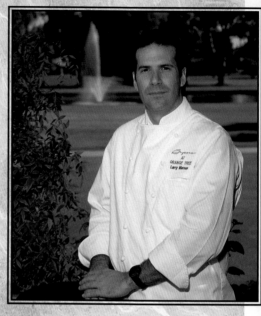

There are a number of reasons why The Orange Tree Golf & Conference Resort is as popular with locals as it is with tourists. The course, which is open to the public, is an excellent one. It is also one of the most lushly planted in the valley. That same landscaping forms a dramatic backdrop for Capers, the major in-house restaurant which has also developed a substantial local following.

The room is designed in an open and airy manner that still manages to feel cozy and intimate thanks to cushy banquettes and impeccable table settings. Live music from the adjacent lounge helps create a sense of big city sophistication.

Capers biggest draw, however, is the exciting food creations of chef Larry Marcus. Growing up in Europe and undergoing an apprenticeship program in Florida under a Certified Master Chef gave Marcus a solid grounding in international cuisine which is clearly reflected in Capers menu.

Dishes such as goat cheese and spinach stuffed veal chop, pistachio and honey mustard-crusted rack of lamb, shrimp Portofino stuffed with crab and sauced with a provolone and tomato mixture as well as lusciously decadent desserts well prove Marcus' words, "Food is an art form that comes from the heart."

Capers: Orange Tree Golf & Conference Resort, 10601 N. 56th St., Scottsdale. 443-2119
(Call for reservations and hours of business.)

Sonoran Spring Roll

Appetizer

Seafood should have a fresh clean aroma when purchased.

1 cup heavy whipping cream
1/2 teaspoon Old Bay seasoning
(available in spice section of most supermarkets)
1/2 teaspoon green chiles, chopped
(canned are fine)
1/4 teaspoon fresh ginger, minced
1/4 teaspoon fresh garlic, minced
1 tablespoon olive oil
4 ounces rock shrimp
4 ounces sea scallops quartered
(or whole bay scallops)

4 ounces crab meat
3 medium mushrooms, sliced
1 green onion, sliced
1 teaspoon brandy (optional)
1/2 cup breadcrumbs
1/4 cup cheddar cheese, grated
1/4 cup jack cheese, grated
1 cup Napa cabbage, finely shredded
1 package rice-based springroll wrappers
1 egg whisked with a little milk

In a saucepan, heat together first 5 ingredients and reduce by half. Set aside. Preheat a skillet with about a tablespoon of olive oil and saute seafood (only until about 3/4ths done), onions and mushrooms. Deglaze pan with brandy if you wish. Chill mixture. Add enough breadcrumbs to seafood mixture to absorb liquid. Add cheeses and cabbage to mixture folding together well. Add enough of the seasoned cream reduction to make mixture moist. Preheat oven to 350.° Lay the egg roll wrapper on work surface with one corner facing you. Place about 1/2 cup filling in middle, fold the bottom and side corners onto the mixture then roll up sealing top edge with eggwash. Repeat. Will make 8 - 12 rolls depending on size of wrapper. Bake until wrappers are golden brown and crisp, about 5 - 7 minutes. Serve with Oriental-style salad if desired.

*Beverage recommendation - Chimney Rock Chardonnay 1995.

Manchego Filet

Entree

The secret to great vegetables is to prepare them al dente. This mixture can accompany chicken or a firm-textured fish as well, just add a spritz of fresh lemon.

1 whole portobello mushroom, grilled until softened
1 small red onion, cut into 3/4 " slices & speared with a toothpick, grilled lightly
1/4 cup garlic cloves, peeled and roasted on the grill in a pie tin
2 medium shallots, quartered and roasted on the grill in a pie tin
1 teaspoon fresh herbs, chopped (parsley, basil, cilantro, etc.)
salt and pepper to taste
1/2 pound manchego cheese, shredded (a hard Spanish variety available at A.J.'s and sometimes Trader Joe's)
2 cups heavy cream reduced by half
4 8-ounce beef filet mignons

Prepare grill and cook vegetables as directed. Dice mushroom and onions and toss with garlic, shallots and herbs. Season to taste.
Grill filets to desired temperature, meanwhile folding the manchego cheese into the cream reduction and heating to incorporate. Serve vegetables and beef on a heated plate and top beef with cheese sauce.

*Beverage recommendation - J.Lohr "Seven Oaks" Cabernet Sauvignon 1994.

Ahi Tuna with Mango Chile Chutney

Entree

Ahi tuna should be a deep red color. Sushi grade Ahi is recommended for those who like their tuna rare.

1/2 cup soy sauce
1/2 cup water
1 tablespoon sesame oil
1/2 teaspoon fresh ginger, minced
4 7-ounce ahi tuna filets

Chutney
1 medium mango, peeled, seeded and diced
1 small red onion, diced
1 small mild Anaheim chile, seeded and diced
1 each tablespoon red and green bell pepper
1 teaspoon fresh mint, chopped fine

In a bowl large enough to hold tuna, mix first 4 ingredients. Marinate tuna in the refrigerator 1 to 1 1/2 hours, turning frequently.

Fold together chutney ingredients and let stand 2 hours.

Prepare grill and cook tuna to desired temperature. Plate and garnish with chutney and, if desired, pickled ginger and wasabi.

*Beverage recommendation - Calera Pinot Noir 1994.

The Orange Tree's Chocolate Spire

Dessert

prepared chocolate sheet cake, about 1/2 inch thick, unfrosted
    vanilla ice cream in rectangular packaging, very firm
1 - 1/2 cups chocolate chips
1/2 cup heavy cream
1/2 cup ounces praline paste (available at A.J.'s)
1/2 cup butterscotch chips
1 square white chocolate, shaved into long curls

Using a round biscuit cutter, or cutting 2 inch squares, cut 16 pieces from the cake. Cut 12 pieces of ice cream, in circles or squares, to match cake, keep frozen. In saucepan bring cream to a boil and pour over chocolate chips. Stir gently to blend. Divide in half. Add praline paste to one half, blend. Add butterscotch chips to other half, blend. Build spires with cake piece on bottom followed by ice cream. Repeat twice for a total of 4 cake layers and 3 ice cream layers of each portion. Store frozen. When time to serve, place each spire in center of chilled plate and drizzle warm sauces over the top. Drape white chocolate curls around each spire.

*Beverage recommendation - Moet & Chandon White Star Champagne.

Different Pointe of View
Jeffrey Beeson
Chef de Cuisine

Jeff Beeson is sitting on top of the world. Or, at the very least, he is overlooking a big chunk of the Valley of the Sun. He heads up the kitchen of Different Pointe of View, THE premiere view restaurant in the city. After dark a breathtaking magic carpet of lights is spread out below and sunset-gazing from one of the lavishly planted terraces is a favorite "wind-down" place for resort guests and valley residents.

The interior of the restaurant is equally spectacular. Warm, desert colors are enhanced by striking contemporary art, handmade quilts and pottery. Rarely are elegance and comfort married so successfully.

Beeson's bold Southwestern-influenced cuisine is perfectly matched to the room. He excels at incorporating classical techniques and indigenous ingredients. Another hallmark of his culinary style is the use of fresh herbs, fruits and vegetables from the 5,200 square foot Chef's Garden that covers a hill adjacent to the restaurant.

Matching wines to Beeson's exciting creations is no challenge. DPOV offers one of the best wine lists in the world and has been a recipient of the "Grand Award" from Wine Spectator Magazine since 1991.

In his off time, the chef plays as hard as he cooks, favoring rock climbing and biking as well as spending time with his wife, Nora and baby daughter, Sydnee.

Different Pointe of View: Pointe Hilton Resort at Tapatio Cliffs, 11111 N. 7th St. Phoenix. 863-0912
(Call for reservations and hours of business.)

Butternut Squash Soup with Pasilla Chiles

Soup

2 tablespoons olive oil
1/4 cup yellow onion, diced
1 tablespoon garlic, chopped
1 teaspoon pasilla chile, chopped
1 cup butternut squash, peeled and cubed
2 cups chicken stock

1 tablespoon molasses
1 cup heavy cream
kosher salt and cracked pepper to taste
1/4 cup pumpkin seeds, toasted (available at Trader Joe's and Hispanic supermarkets)
1 tablespoon pasilla chile, chopped

Heat olive oil in a skillet. Saute onion, garlic, chile and squash until soft. Add the chicken stock and simmer 15 to 20 minutes or until squash is soft. Add the remaining ingredients and simmer until the cream has thickened. Puree, strain and season to taste. Ladle into four soup bowls and sprinkle pumpkin seeds and chopped chiles on top.

*Beverage recommendation - your favorite beer.

Pork Tenderloin Marinated in Dark Beer with Candied Nectarine and Onion Sauce and Creamy Yellow Grits

Entree

4 6-ounce pork tenderloins
1 12-ounce Modelo Negro beer
1 cup corn oil
4 serrano peppers, sliced

4 cloves garlic, crushed
1 cup soy sauce
1 tablespoon chopped cilantro

Combine last 6 ingredients in a deep bowl. Marinate the pork in mixture overnight in the refrigerator.

Nectarine and Onion Sauce

1 tablespoon olive oil
1/2 cup red onion, julienned
1 tablespoon garlic
1/4 cup beets, peeled and finely diced
1 cup nectarines, diced

1/4 cup honey
1/8 cup sugar
1 1/2 cups chicken stock
1/4 cup raspberry vinegar

Heat oil in a skillet, saute the onions, garlic and beets until soft. Add sugar and simmer over low heat until onions carmelize. Add remaining ingredients and reduce by one half. Strain and set aside.

Grits

2 cups chicken stock
1 cup coarse yellow grits
1 cup jalapeno Jack cheese, grated

1 tablespoon poblano chiles, chopped
1 tablespoon yellow onions, chopped
1 teaspoon garlic, chopped

Bring stock to boil. Add grits & stir until slightly thickened. Add remaining ingredients & cook until grits are soft but still creamy. Hold in double boiler over hot water.

Assembly

Remove pork from marinade and grill until medium rare to medium. Allow to rest 5 minutes. Spoon approximately 1 cup grits on each of four plates. Place tenderloin next to grits and ladle with sauce. Garnish with fresh herbs.

*Beverage recommendation - Modelo Negro beer.

Grilled Porterhouse Steak with Tangy Plum Ketchup, Potatoes au Gratin and Corn and Red Onion Relish

Entree

4 16 to 18-ounce Porterhouse steaks   kosher salt and cracked pepper

Tangy Plum Ketchup

1 tablespoon olive oil
1 tablespoon garlic, chopped
1 tablespoon onion, diced
1 tablespoon poblano chile, diced
1 cup fresh plums, pitted and julienned
1/2 cup tomatoes, peeled, seeded and diced
1/2 cup raisins

1/2 cup light corn syrup
1/2 cup malt vinegar
1 tablespoon tomato paste
1/2 teaspoon cumin
1/2 teaspoon turmeric
1/2 teaspoon pure red chile powder
kosher salt and cracked pepper

Heat olive oil in a skillet. Saute garlic, onions and poblanos until soft. Add plums, tomatoes and raisins and simmer until soft. Add remaining ingredients and simmer 25 - 30 more minutes. Puree, strain and hold at room temperature.

Corn and Red Onion Relish

1 cup fresh corn kernels, roasted in
    a 450° oven for 25 - 30 minutes
1/8 cup red onion, diced
1 tablespoon garlic, chopped
1 tablespoon poblano chile, diced
1 tablespoon lime juice
kosher salt and cracked pepper to taste

1 cup smoked cheddar, grated
kosher salt, cracked pepper and Tabasco
sauce to taste.
2 large russet potatoes, sliced
1/4 cup breadcrumbs
1/4 cup parmesan, grated

Combine all ingredients and hold until serving.

Potato and Smoked Cheddar Au Gratin

1 tablespoon olive oil
1 tablespoon garlic, chopped
1 tablespoon shallots, chopped

2 tablespoons onion, chopped
1/2 cup chicken stock
1 cup heavy cream

Preheat oven to 350 F. Heat oil in a skillet. Saute garlic, shallots and onion until soft. Add chicken stock and cream, reduce by half. Add cheddar slowly, season to taste and reduce until thickened. Place the sliced potatoes in a casserole dish and pour the sauce over the potatoes. Cover and bake 35 to 40 minutes or until potatoes are soft. Uncover, sprinkle with breadcrumbs and parmesan and bake an additional 20 to 25 minutes or until potatoes are soft and top is golden brown. Keep warm.

Assembly

Grill the Porterhouse steaks to desired temperature. Place each steak in the center of large plate. Top each with a scoop of potatoes. Put a dollop of Tangy Plum Ketchup to one side, a portion of Corn and Red Onion Relish on the other. Garnish with fresh herbs.

*Beverage recommendation - red Zinfandel.

Chayote Squash and Carrot Cake with Ancho ChileHoney

Dessert

1 1/2 cups chayote squash, peeled and grated
1 1/2 cups carrots, grated
1 cup sugar

(continued on page 151)

Drinkwater's
Travis Vierthaler
Executive Chef

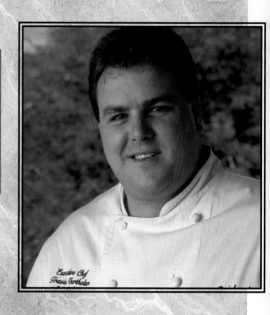

There was a time when restaurants in the far North Valley were as scarce as the proverbial poultry tooth. Known then as Oaxaca, this was one of the exceptions. A spectacular view, comfortable surroundings and hearty American fare pulled folks from both Carefree and Scottsdale.

Major changes have taken place in the last few years. Now, the area is booming. The restaurant's name has been changed, honoring much loved former Scottsdale mayor, Herb Drinkwater. Talented young chef Travis Vierthaler is heading the kitchen, and he has brought the cuisine up mega-notches. The restaurant currently pulls diners from all over the valley. The only thing that remains the same is that sparkling city lights view.

Vierthaler is an Arizona native, born and raised in Flagstaff to parents who consider food an art form. He has an intrinsic flair for regional American cooking which is reflected in Drinkwater's menu. Dishes such as salmon Santa Fe, Southwestern chicken and crispy crabcakes have them coming back to Drinkwater's for more.

The proud daddy of a young son, Alexander, Vierthaler finds he craves the exotic when he dines out, especially East Indian and Oriental food.

Drinkwater's: 8711 E. Pinnacle Peak Rd., Scottsdale.
998-2222
(Call for reservations and hours of business.)

Wild Mushroom Risotto Cakes
with Seafood in Parmesan Cream Sauce

Appetizer

1 cup butter
5 cups arborio rice
1 cup yellow onion, diced
2 quarts chicken stock, hot
1 1/2 cups parmesan cheese,
  fresh grated
1 teaspoon white pepper

1 cup shiitake mushrooms, stemmed,
  sliced and sauteed
corn meal as needed
2 tablespoons olive oil
8 jumbo scallops
8 green lip mussels on the half shell
parmesan cream sauce (see recipe below)

Parmesan Cream Sauce

2 cups heavy cream
1 cup parmesan cheese, fresh grated
salt and pepper to taste
In a small saucepan, bring cream and cheese to a boil, stirring constantly.
Reduce until volume of sauce is about 2 cups. Set aside and keep warm.

In a large saucepan, melt butter and saute rice and onions until rice is translucent. Be careful not to burn the rice. Add hot chicken stock to rice 2 cups at a time, stirring to incorporate all liquid before adding the next batch. Add parmesan, shiitakes and white pepper and stir. Let rice cool. Form 8 patties out of the rice mixture. Dredge in cornmeal. Heat oil in skillet and fry patties until crisp. Set aside. Add more oil to pan if needed and quickly saute scallops and mussels being careful not to overcook. Place 2 cakes on each of 4 plates. Place two scallops and 2 mussels on each pancake. Drizzle sauce over all and serve at once.

*Beverage recommendation - Chardonnay.

Key West Shrimp with Sweet Vegetable Saute

Entree

2 tablespoons olive oil
20 extra jumbo shrimp, peeled and deveined
6 limes, zested and juiced
4 oranges, zested and juiced
2 lemons, zested and juiced
2 baby zucchini, cut in 3 inch long, 1/16 inch wide matchsticks
2 carrots, peeled and cut as above
2 large red bell peppers, peeled and cut as above
1 cup lemon juice
1 cup sugar
1 pound angel hair pasta, cooked al dente and drained

Heat oil in a skillet and sautee shrimp until 3/4's done. Add sugar, lemon juice, citrus juice, citrus zest, vegetables, lemon juice and sugar. Cook briefly to heat through, about 2 - 3 minutes. Remove from heat and toss with angel hair pasta. Serve immediately.

*Beverage recommendation - Riesling or Gewurztraminer.

Roast Duck with Sundried Cranberry and Walnut Cabernet Sauce

Entree

Either rice or pasta is a good accompaniment.

2 5-pound ducks
3 tablespoons kosher or sea salt

2 tablespoons black pepper
2 tablespoons thyme

Preheat oven to 350° Combine salt, pepper and thyme and rub on ducks. Place ducks on a baking pan and slow roast about one hour or until internal temperature reaches 165° Remove from oven and set aside to cool. Meanwhile prepare sauce.

Sauce

1 cup honey
2 cups cabernet
1 cup sundried cranberries

1 cup walnuts
2 tablespoons butter

Combine honey and cabernet in a medium saucepan and bring to a boil. Simmer until total volume equals about 1 1/2 cups. Add cranberries, walnuts and butter. Stir until butter is melted.

Assembly

Cut each duck in half lengthwise. Remove bones from breast region and place half of duck on each plate. Drizzle with sauce.

*Beverage recommendation - Cabernet Sauvignon.

Jack Daniels Caramel Bread Pudding

Dessert

1 1/2 pounds white bread (chef prefers a crusty French), in 1/4 inch cubes
2 cups brown sugar
1 cup granulated sugar
5 tablespoons cinnamon
10 large eggs

4 cups walnuts
2 cups raisins
1 quart half and half
1 quart heavy cream
Jack Daniels sauce (see recipe below)
whipped cream

Preheat oven to 350° Mix all ingredients together and place in a 8 x 10 x 4 inch baking pan. Bake for 45 minutes. Refrigerate overnight.

Sauce

2 cups prepared caramel sauce (Smucker's, etc.)
1 cup Jack Daniels

Combine in saucepan and heat through.

Cut bread pudding into 3 inch squares and heat in the microwave. Pour warm Jack Daniels sauce over each serving and top with whipped cream.

*Beverage recommendation - Jack Daniels and coffee.

Franco's
Trattoria
Franco Fazzuoli - *Chef/Owner*
Steve Martin - *Partner*

As far as many Valley diners are concerned, Franco Fazzuoli wrote the book on regional Italian cuisine. The charming Florentine was the first to introduce authentic Tuscan specialties on his menu when he opened the original Franco's in 1987. In a very short time, his tiny restaurant could no longer handle the throngs of eager customers.

After moving to his present location, a spacious enclave that neatly combines sophistication and comfort, Fazzuoli took on Steve Martin as his partner. The two prepare everything served in the restaurant fresh and from scratch - breads, pastas, dressings and sauces. Pastry chef Julie Kinnard is responsible for the delectable desserts. The trio's food is characterized by impeccable preparation and clean, colorful presentations.

Fazzuoli trained in his native Italy and after moving to New York, headed up some of the best known restaurants in Manhattan. When it came time to raise a family, he and his wife Caroline, a former ballet dancer, made the decision to move to Phoenix. He has seen to it that Martin, a natural and instinctive cook, has the opportunity to frequently visit Italy to travel and train.

When the restaurant is closed, Fazzuoli can be found enjoying the company of his two young daughters. Martin brushes up on his Italian, hikes in the desert and restores old cars.

❦ A cooking tip from Franco: "When cooking pasta, add a little olive oil to the water to keep noodles from sticking, but never to the finished pasta or sauce will not cling."

Franco's Trattoria:
8120 N. Hayden Rd., Scottsdale.
948-6655
(Call for reservations and hours of business.)

Crostini

Appetizer

1/4 pound chicken livers
1 tablespoon unsalted butter
1 tablespoon olive oil
2 tablespoons onion, chopped
1 bay leaf

1 anchovy, drained and chopped
1 teaspoon capers, drained and chopped
1 cup chicken stock, heated
4 slices (1/4 inch thick) Tuscan bread

Rinse the chicken livers and cut away any yellow spots. Heat the butter and oil in a saute pan over medium-low heat. Add the livers and onion and saute 3 - 5 minutes. Stir in the bay leaf. Remove the livers and finely chop. Combine with capers and anchovys. Return mixture to the pan and add a little chicken stock. Cook 1 - 2 minutes longer.

Toast the bread lightly and let cool completely. Dip each slice into the remaining warm chicken stock just to coat. Discard the bay leaf and spread liver mixture atop.

*Beverage recommendation - Mastroberardino Fiano di Avellino Radici di Latio

Veal Chop Mostarda

Entree

1/4 cup olive oil
4 10-ounce veal loin chops
1/4 pound fresh shiitake mushrooms, sliced
1/4 pound oyster mushrooms, sliced
1/2 cup brandy
3 tablespoons good-quality mustard
3/4 cup heavy cream
1/2 cup veal or chicken stock
1 tablespoon butter

Preheat oven to 450° F. Heat olive oil in a large saute pan and brown chops on both sides. Transfer chops to a baking dish and bake about 6 - 8 minutes in the oven while preparing sauce. To the saute pan, add the shiitake and oyster mushrooms and saute briefly. On medium-low heat, add brandy all at once. Light the mixture to burn off alcohol (use caution). Once the flames have subsided, add mustard to the pan and stir. Add the cream and stock and reduce sauce to desired consistency. Swirl in butter to finish. (If the sauce begans to separate, add a little more stock.) Place a chop on each plate and ladle sauce evenly over each.

Beverage recommendation - Either Beringer or Mondavi Chardonnay Reserve

Risotto Funghi Porcini

Entree

1/4 cup extra virgin olive oil
6 cloves garlic, crushed
3/4 cup onion, chopped
1 cup Arborio rice
  (available in the gourmet
  section of the supermarket)
2 cups roma tomatoes, chopped

2 ounces dry porcini mushrooms,
  reconstituted with soaking liquid
  strained and reserved
6 cup chicken stock
2 tablespoons butter
salt and fresh ground black pepper
parmesan cheese, grated

Heat olive oil in a medium saucepan and cook garlic until golden. Add onion and saute 1 minute. Add the rice and cook 1 minute longer. Add the tomatoes, mushrooms and 1 tablespoon reserved liquid and stir. Add 2 cups chicken broth and bring to a boil, stirring frequently to keep rice from sticking. Lower the heat and gradually add remaining stock 1 cup at a time, waiting for liquid to be absorbed after each addition. Cook until the rice is al dente. Mix in the butter and salt and pepper to taste. Top with parmesan cheese.

*Beverage recommendation - Antinori Tignenello

Torta Di Riso E Nocciole

Dessert
Rice and Hazelnut Cake

4 cups whole milk
1/2 cup granulated sugar
1 vanilla bean, split
1/2 cup Arborio rice
1/2 cup hazelnuts, skinned and toasted

1/2 cup granulated sugar
2 large eggs
2 tablespoons Frangelico liqueur
3 large egg whites
1/4 cup granulated sugar
whipped cream or confectioners sugar

Preheat oven to 350° F. Grease and flour a parchment lined 9 inch springform pan. In a medium saucepan, combine the milk, 1/2 cup sugar and vanilla bean and bring to a boil. Add the rice and lower heat to a simmer. Cook the rice 35 - 40 minutes, stirring frequently, until most of the liquid is absorbed. Scrape the seeds from the vanilla bean into the rice and discard pod. Transfer the mixture to a shallow bowl and cool to room temperature. Grind the nuts with 1/2 cup sugar in a food processor until very fine. Add this mixture to the cooled rice along with the eggs and liqueur. In a mixer bowl, beat the whites until thick and foamy, gradually adding the 1/4 cup of sugar. Beat just until stiff peaks form. Fold the whites into the rice mixture in three additions. Transfer mixture into the prepared pan and bake 40 - 45 minutes until golden brown and a cake tester inserted into the center comes out clean. Cool cake completely and garnish with sweetened whipped cream or dust with confectioners sugar.

Pistachios and rum can be substituted for the hazelnuts and Frangelico.

*Beverage recommendation - Vin Santo

Gianni
Ristorante-Bar-Pizzeria
Gianni Scovenna - *Owner*
Dwight Wintringer
Executive Chef

Gianni Scovenna originally made his mark on the Valley dining scene with his very succesful Northern Italian restaurant on Hayden Road. Now, he is back, in a larger space just a few miles east.

It is exceptionally attractive, spacious but divided into several intimate dining areas and decorated with colorful folkloric murals. As always though, with Gianni's restaurants, the cuisine is the main event.

Scovenna's signature is exceptionally fresh and light food, the kind he grew up on in the small town near Milan where he was born. "It is simple food," he says. "but it stands on its own because of the quality."

He and chef Dwight Wintringer, formerly with the **renowned** Spavones Seven Hills Italian restaurant in Chicago, have designed a menu that showcases fresh seafood, chicken and veal dishes, made-on-the-premises pastas and gnocchi. Also featured are risottos and imaginative pizzas.

Scovenna and Wintringer are dedicated to providing extremely personal service to customers. And, they manage to have personal lives as well. Both are married and raising small children.

Gianni: 10155 E. Via Linda, Scottsdale.
657-0818
(Call for reservations and hours of business.)

Stracciatella

Soup

This is a great "starter" or good as a meal on its own. The light broth laced with spinach and egg needs a hearty piece of Tuscan bread as an accompaniment.

8 cups chicken broth, fresh or canned
8 cups fresh spinach, cleaned and chopped
4 eggs, cracked and yolks just broken
salt and white pepper to taste

In a saucepan, bring the broth and spinach to a low boil. With a whisk, slowly swirl in eggs one at a time, being careful to incorporate fully. Add salt and pepper.

*Beverage recommendation - Moretti beer.

Chicken Vesuvio

Entree

The chicken should be kept moist and in the sauce while cooking in order to absorb all the flavors. Warning - not for those who shy away from garlic!

2 3-pound chickens, quartered
4 potatoes, peeled and quartered lengthwise
4 tablespoons butter, melted
4 tablespoons butter
4 tablespoons olive oil
1/4 cup garlic, chopped (garlic lovers can feel free to add more)
4 cups chicken broth (fresh or canned)
2 cups white wine
1/4 cup minced parsley
generous pinch of oregano (rub it between your palms to release flavor)
salt and pepper to taste

Preheat oven to 375° Coat potatoes and chicken with melted butter, place in pan and bake about 30 minutes. Set aside. Meanwhile, in a skillet, heat butter and oil. Add garlic and saute until golden-brown. Add wine, broth, parsley, oregano and salt and pepper and heat through. Pour over chicken and potatoes and bake about 45 minutes or until chicken is done and liquid has reduced to sauce consistency. Remove chicken and potatoes to a heated platter and pour sauce over all.

*Beverage recommendation - Santa Margherita Pinot Grigio 1995.

Penne Salsa Cruda

Appetizer

This Heart Smart dish is very rich in color and flavor. It can be served either hot or cold.

20 roma tomatoes, chopped (not too small)
1 cup onion, chopped
1/4 cup fresh basil, chopped
1/4 cup garlic, chopped
20 kalamata olives, pitted and chopped

4 teaspoon capers, drained
1/2 cup olive oil
salt, pepper and red chile flakes
(optional) to taste
1 pound penne pasta

In a medium bowl, combine tomatoes, onions, basil, garlic, olives, capers and olive oil. Add seasonings and let sit in the refrigerator 1 hour. Just prior to serving, cook pasta to desired firmness. While pasta is cooking, place the sauce in a pan and heat through. Drain pasta and toss with the sauce, cooking a little longer so flavors develop.

*Beverage recommendation - Principessa Gavi, 1994.

Veal Vogherese

Entree

This dish originates in Voghere where peppers grow abundantly. The flavor is wonderfully sweet and rustic.

4 6-ounce slices veal from the leg
flour for dredging
4 tablespoons butter
4 tablespoons olive oil
1 tablespoon garlic, chopped
2 cups green peppers, cut in 1 inch pieces
2 cups red peppers, cut in 1 inch pieces
2 cups yellow peppers, cut in 1 inch pieces
2 cups white wine
4 cups chicken broth
salt and pepper to taste

Pound veal gently with a meat mallet (it helps to sprinkle the veal with a little water and wrap it in plastic wrap to prevent sticking). Dust veal with flour and set aside. In skillet, heat butter and oil and cook garlic until golden brown. Add veal to the pan and lightly brown both sides. Add peppers and toss with veal. Deglaze pan with wine and broth. Add salt and pepper and cook about 20 minutes or until sauce has reduced by half. Arrange veal on heated platter and pour sauce over all.

*Beverage recommendation - Travalini Gattinara, 1992.

Griff's
Merv Griffin's
Wickenburg Inn
Gabriel Lujan
Executive Chef

With development everywhere, the real West is a disappearing commodity. But not out Wickenburg way. Surrounded by 4,700 acres of untouched High Sonoran desert, Merv Griffin's Wickenburg Inn is a national treasure.

For those seeking authentic Western hospitality there is simply no better place to find it. Here is the opportunity to ride the range with working cowpokes, participate in cattle drives, take lessons in roping, barrel racing and other rodeo competitions. Or, for those so inclined, there is tennis, nearby golf and two swimming pools for lounging.

No matter how guests spend their day at the Inn, mealtime is equally anticipated by everyone. And no wonder. Chef Gabe Lujan specializes in irresistibly hearty, big-flavored Western-style food. A native Westerner from Durango, Colorado, Lujan insists on the use of fresh, wholesome ingredients and "scratch" preparation of everything served at the Inn. Lujan's signature dishes include "Bourbonqued" ribs, honey-chile glazed pink Western trout and salsa slaw with a kick from jalapeno peppers.

Gabe is a man at the right place, one of his favorite leisure activities is horseback riding.

Griff's: 8 miles north of Wickenburg on State Route 89 (Prescott Highway), 1-800-Wickenburg
(Call for reservations and hours of business.)

Appetizer

1/2 pound feta cheese
1/2 pound cream cheese
2 - 3 jalapeno peppers, fine dice
1/2 red onion, fine dice

4 10-inch flour tortillas
toothpicks
oil for frying
salsa (see recipe below)
guacamole (purchased or your favorite recipes)

Chipotle Salsa

10 roma tomatoes, cored and cut in half
1 medium yellow onion, cut in half
4 green onions
4 garlic cloves

1/2 tablespoon cumin powder
1/2 small can chipotle peppers (Embasa brand can generally be found in the supermarket Mexican food aisle)
salt and pepper to taste

Prepare barbecue and grill vegetables long enough to soften and obtain char marks. Cool and combine with rest of ingredients in a blender or food processer. Puree, Correct seasonings and chill.

Assembly

Let cheese soften, and combine with jalapenos and red onion. Warm tortillas 2 at a time. Cut into quarters. Place a spoonful of cheese mixture at the wide end of the triangle and roll up making sure all cheese is inside the tortilla. Repeat until you have 8 wraps. Toothpick securely and freeze. In a deep fryer or wok, heat oil and fry blossoms a few at a time until golden brown (Don't overcook or they open and lose the filling). Drain and serve with guacamole and salsa.

*Beverage recommendation - Margarita.

Vegetable Chilaquiles Casserole

Entree

Along with a green salad, this makes a great vegetarian meal. It is also a good accompaniment for the flank steak.

4 - 5 large cloves garlic, unpeeled
2 large red peppers
2 large green peppers
2 large yellow peppers
4 medium poblano peppers
3 - 4 ears fresh corn, husked
4 medium yellow squash, cut lengthwise in 1/4 inch strips
4 medium zucchini, cut lengthwise in 1/4 inch strips

1 pound ricotta cheese
1 pound monterey jack cheese, grated (reserve 1 cup)
1 tablespoon oregano
1/2 tablespoon cumin
salt and pepper to taste
2 cups chunky salsa (prepared or homemade)
2 dozen corn tortillas

Prepare barbecue. Wrap garlic cloves in square of foil and place on grill. Roast whole peppers until blistered, remove from grill and place in paper or plastic bag. Roast corn until softened and slightly browned. Remove from grill. Grill squash until slightly charred. Remove along with garlic which should be soft. Peel, seed and cut peppers into strips. Cut kernels from corn. Meanwhile, in a mixing bowl combine cheeses with seasonings and roasted garlic squeezed from skin. Take a cast iron pan and oil. Start with overlapping tortillas. Spread with cheese mixture. Top with some zucchini, peppers and roasted corn. Moisten with salsa. Repeat twice more, sprinkling top with reserved jack cheese. Cover tightly with a lid or aluminum foil. Replace on grill over low heat and bake one hour. Let casserole rest about 15 - 20 minutes before serving. (May be made in advance and heated before serving.)

*Beverage recommendation - Fruit flavored iced tea.

Southwest Marinated Flank Steak

Entree

2 pound flank steak
1/2 cup Worcestershire sauce
1/4 cup soy sauce
2 tablespoons liquid smoke
1 tablespoon red chile powder

1 teaspoon white pepper
2 - 4 cloves garlic, chopped
1/2 tablespoon fresh ground black pepper
1/2 tablespoon cumin powder

Combine all liquids and spices and allow to sit for 10 minutes. Place flank steak in a pan or bowl large enough that the marinade will cover it. Pour marinade over, making sure meat is fully submerged. Refrigerate overnight.

Prepare barbecue. Remove steak from marinade and grill to desired temperature. Flank steak should be cut thinly and on the diagonal.

*Beverage recommendation - Fat Tire Amber Ale.

Fire-Roasted Vegetable Quesadilla

Salad

This makes an interesting, off-beat salad or first course and can be served warm or cold.

5 roma tomatoes, cored and diced
1 zucchini, split lengthwise and sliced
   about 1/4 inch thick
2 yellow squash, split lengthwise and
   sliced about 1/4 inch thick
1 red pepper, split lengthwise,
   seeds removed
1 yellow pepper, split lengthwise,
   seeds removed
1 green pepper, split lengthwise,
   seeds removed
1 poblano chile, split lengthwise,
   seeds removed
2 ears fresh corn, husked

1/4 cup vegetable or olive oil
1/2 tablespoon dried thyme
1/2 tablespoon, dried oregano
1 teaspoon cumin powder
1 tablespoon red chile powder
2 cloves garlic, chopped
salt and pepper to taste
4 10-inch flour tortillas
1 tablespoon fresh thyme, chopped
1 tablespoon fresh oregano, chopped
1/8 cup balsamic vinegar
2 cups cheddar, feta or your favorite
   cheese, shredded or crumbled

Prepare barbecue. Combine oil, dried herbs and garlic and mix well. Evenly coat all vegetables except corn and tomatoes with oil mixture. Grill veggies, one kind at a time, until all are softened and have brown grill marks. Remove from grill and let cool. Roast corn lightly. Remove, cool and cut off kernels. Dice rest of grilled vegetables to the same size as the tomatoes. Combine all vegetables together in a bowl with the fresh herbs and balsamic vinegar. Hold at room temperature or chill, according to preference.

On warm grill, heat and crisp up flour tortillas. Top with tepid or chilled veggie mix and cheese. Garnish with fresh cilantro and sliced avocado if desired. Serve with chipotle salsa (see recipe above).

*Beverage recommendation - Tequila Sunrise.

HOPS!
Bistro & Brewery
Alan Skversky
Executive Chef & General Manager

Hops! blazed the micro-brewery trail in Arizona, introducing the unbeatable combination of sophisticated contemporary surroundings, adept service, premium hand-crafted beers and the exciting cuisine of chef Alan Skversky. The restaurants are magnets for locals who are equally enthused about fine brews and full-flavored food.

Skversky, a native of Philadelphia and graduate of the Culinary Institute of America, is a pioneer in the art of pairing beers and foods as well as an expert in beer cookery, one of the fastest growing culinary trends in the country. He is in great demand nationally as a speaker on the subject.

Not surprisingly, Skversky designed Hops! menu to showcase the best of both the brewmasters art and food. Drawing on influences that range from Southwestern and Mediterranean to Oriental, Skversky incorporates beer into dishes such as spicy Red Ale shrimp, beer-battered fish and chips and Philly cheese steak sandwich with beer-braised onions. The service staff is well-trained in helping matching the distinctive beers to the various menu offerings.

When customers fall in love with one of Hops! beers, they also have the convenient option of ordering it to go in a jug or keg at the Shea Blvd. store.

Hops! Bistro & Brewery:
2584 E. Camelback Rd. (Biltmore Fashion Park), Phoenix. 468-0500
8668 E. Shea Blvd., Scottsdale. 998-7777
Scottsdale Fashion Square location will reopen in late 1998.
(Call for reservations and hours of business.)

Sesame Seared Ahi
with Wheat Beer Aioli and Wasabi Cream

Appetizer

The banana/clove character of the unfiltered wheat beer compliments the nutty flavor of the tuna & the spiciness of the wasabi. The pickled cucumbers should be prepared a day ahead for maximum flavor.

1/2 lb sushi grade Ahi tuna
1/2 cup black and white sesame seeds
3 tablespoons sesame oil
radish sprouts

pickled cucumbers (see recipe below)
Wheat Beer aioli (see recipe below)
wasabi cream (see recipe below)

Pickled Cucumbers

1 cucumber, split lengthwise and deseeded
1/2 small yellow onion, julienned

1/2 cup rice wine vinegar
3 tablespoons sugar
salt and pepper to taste

Toss all ingredients in a bowl and refrigerate overnite.

Wheat Beer Aioli

1 cup mayonnaise
2 tablespoons roasted and minced garlic

2 teaspoons lemon juice
1/2 cup wheat beer

Blend all ingredients well.

Wasabi Cream

1/4 cup wasabi powder (available at Cost Plus and other specialty and gourmet markets)
1/2 cup heavy cream

Blend well and adjust to taste.

Assembly

Preferably the night before preparation, coat Ahi in sesame seeds and refrigerate. (It helps the seeds cling.) Heat oil in a skillet. Place tuna in skillet and cook evenly on both sides, approximately one minute. (The object is to evenly cook the exterior and leave the center red and rare.) Thinly slice tuna and arrange 4-5 slices on each plate. Garnish with radish sprouts and drained pickled cucumbers. Drizzle with aioli and wasabi cream and sprinkle with remaining sesame seeds

*Beverage recommendation - Hops! Wheat beer.

RaspberryChipotle Glazed DuckBreast
with Carrot Jalapeño Mousse

Entree

Bold sweet and spicy flavors stand up well to crisp-seared duck breast. Easy to prepare ahead of time or ala minute, this dish is sure to please all palates.

4 trimmed fresh duck breasts
1/4 cup pureed chipotle chiles

1 cup raspberry beer
1/2 cup sugar

In a hot skillet, sear duck breast skin side down for approximately three minutes on each side. Pour off any fat. Add sugar to pan and cook, stirring constantly until carmelized. Deglaze pan with the beer, add chiles, cover and simmer until a syrupy glaze is formed and coats the duck. Spoon equal amounts of sauce on each plate. Cut each duck breast into thin slices and fan pieces over sauce. Place mousse across from the duck.

Carrot Jalapeno Mousse

6 carrots, peeled, roughly cut and
  boiled until soft
4 jalapeno chile peppers, stemmed,
  seeded and boiled with carrots

1 cup heavy cream
4 whole eggs
salt and pepper to taste
1/2 teaspoon ground nutmeg (fresh ground if possible)

Preheat oven to 300.˚ Puree carrots and jalapenos. Place in bowl and add remaining ingredients. Fold together. Divide mixture evenly into 4 ovenproof ramekins and bake in a water bath for 1 hour. Remove from oven and with paring knife, gently loosen around edge. Invert on each plate.

*Beverage recommendation - Hops! Golden Ale.

Salmon and Shrimp Mousse Potstickers
with Gingered Mashed Potatoes and Plum Sauce

Entree

East meets West in this popular Hops! specialty. The hominess of the mashed potatoes with just a whisper of ginger is a welcome accompaniment to what we call a "potsticker". The crispy wonton shell keeps the fish moist and tender and the mousse creamy and fluffy.

4 7-ounce salmon filets
4 large wonton wrappers, dusted
  with cornstarch
shrimp mousse (see recipe below)

bottled plum sauce (available at Cost Plus, in Asian markets or the gourmet section of the supermarket)
mashed potatoes (see recipe below)

Shrimp Mousse

8 ounces cleaned shrimp
1 egg white
1 tablespoon water chestnuts
1 whole egg

1/2 teaspoon fresh ginger, grated
2 tablespoons heavy cream
salt and pepper to taste

Place all ingredients in a chilled food processor bowl and blend well.

Potatoes

2 pounds potatoes, peeled and quartered
2 cups half and half
1/4 cup butter

3 tablespoons fresh ginger, grated
salt and pepper to taste

Boil and drain potatoes. Heat together the cream, butter and ginger. Add to potatoes and mash. Season with salt and pepper and keep warm.

Assembly

Pre-heat oven to 350°. Butterfly each salmon filet. Lay some mousse in the center and fold back together. Place the mousse-filled salmon in a large wonton wrapper, sealing the edges with a little water. Heat a small amount of oil in skillet and pan sear on all sides. Finish in the oven, approximately 8 minutes.

Divide the mashed potatoes evenly on 4 plates and place a wonton atop. Serve with plum sauce.

*Beverage recommendation - Hops! Raspberry Ale.

Fresh Berries with Raspberry Zabaglione

Dessert

A new twist to this classic makes this dessert a light finish which compliments any meal.

8 egg yolks
1/2 cup sugar
1/2 cup raspberry beer
1 cup heavy cream
4 cups fresh berries, cleaned, washed, dried and evenly divided into 4 goblets

Over a double boiler, briskly whip yolks, sugar and beer until cooked and fluffy. Cool. Whip heavy cream until soft peaks form. Fold into egg mixture. Spoon equally over berries.

*Beverage recommendation - Hops! Stout.

Jade Palace

Davelon Mei
Owner

Davelon Mei literally grew up in the restaurant business, working his way through high school in New York City's prestigious Crown Palace restaurant group. By the age of 18, he was already a manager and knew what his career path would be.

After a move to California, Mei went to work at The Plum Tree restaurants in Los Angeles. There, he developed the idea of opening his own restaurant in Phoenix.

"I was fortunate to be able to draw experienced staff from both New York and Los Angeles for Jade Palace." he says.

Mei designed the restaurant which has an attractive contemporary flair enhanced by soft tones of mauve and grey. His primary point of pride, however, is the food.

Says Mei, "We use the very best of ingredients." House specialties include Filet Mignon with Jumbo Shrimp and General Tso's Chicken. Jade Palace has an excellent wine list and the well-trained staff excels at helping diners match appropriate foods and beverages.

❦ A tip from Davelon -"To get the thinnest possible slices of beef - freeze the meat slightly before cutting to firm it up."

Jade Palace: 9160 E. Shea Blvd., Scottsdale. 391-0607.
(Call for reservations and hours of business.)
Also, opening in October at 1949 W. Ray Rd., Chandler. 855-3338.

Vegetarian Spring Rolls

Appetizer

A spicy treat served with chile oil for dipping.

4 spring roll wrappers (available in Oriental groceries and many supermarket
   produce sections)
3 Chinese black mushrooms (you may substitute fresh or dried, reconstituted
   shiitakes), sliced thin
1/4 cup carrots, shredded
1/4 cup celery, finely diced
2 cups cabbage, shredded
couple drops sesame oil
salt, white pepper and sugar to taste
1 cup vegetable oil

In a mixing bowl, combine mushrooms, carrot, celery, cabbage, sesame oil
and seasonings. Lay out spring roll wrappers and divide mixture evenly
between them. Fold over the ends and roll up, sealing seam with a bit of
water. Heat oil to bubbling in a saute pan and fry rolls until golden brown
and crispy.

*Beverage recommendation - Gewurztraminer.

Crispy Beef

Entree

Delicious over fluffy, steamed white rice.

1 pound boneless sirloin, sliced very thin (about 1/8 inch thick)
flour to coat
1/2 cup vegetable oil
4 green onions, white part only, chopped fine
2 small dried red chiles (or teaspoon red pepper flakes)
1/2 teaspoon fresh ginger, grated
1 tablespoon dried, reconstituted tangerine peel, thinly sliced (available in
   Oriental markets and specialty grocery stores)
1/2 cup water
1 teaspoon soy sauce
1 teaspoon sugar
1/2 teaspoon white vinegar

Dredge beef in flour. Heat oil in skillet until very hot. Fry beef until brown
and crispy. Remove meat from pan and drain. Pour off all but a tablespoon
of oil from pan and reheat. Add onions, peppers, chiles, ginger and tangerine peel and stir for about 10 seconds. Add water, soy sauce, sugar and
vinegar and stir over medium heat until sauce thickens slightly. Add beef,
heat through and serve.

*Beverage recommendation - either chilled Tsing Tao beer or a good Pinot Noir.

Hawaii Five-O

Entree

Microwaving the snowpeas and carrots ahead of time makes this go quickly.

1/4 pound filet mignon, sliced into 4 pieces
1 small chicken breast, sliced into 4 pieces
1 lobster tail, sliced into 4 pieces
4 jumbo shrimp
2 tablespoons vegetable oil
1 clove garlic, chopped fine
pinch of fresh ginger, grated
2 green onions, white part only, chopped fine
8 snow peas, steamed until tender
1 carrot, cut thinly on the diagonal, steamed until tender
4 baby corn, drained
8 slices of water chestnuts
1/2 cup water
dash sesame oil
1 teaspoon soy sauce
2 teaspoons dry white wine or vermouth
salt and white pepper to taste
4 pineapple rings and 4 maraschino cherries (optional garnish)

Heat oil in a skillet. Add garlic, ginger and onion and stir for 5 - 10 seconds. Add chicken and beef and stir for about 1 minute. Add lobster and shrimp and stir another minute. Add vegetables, water, sesame oil, soy sauce, wine and salt and pepper. Cover and cook another 2 minutes. (Add cornstarch to thicken sauce if desired.) Divide between 4 plates and garnish with pineapple ring and cherry.

*Beverage recommendation - Chardonnay.

Sesame Bananas

Dessert

4 ripe but firm bananas, cut into quarters
4 teaspoons flour
2 egg whites
water
2 cups vegetable oil
honey
2 tablespoons toasted sesame seeds

Combine flour and egg white in a bowl, adding water a bit at a time until a stiff batter forms. Heat oil in a pot. Dip banana pieces in batter and fry until golden brown. Drain on paper towel. Arrange on 4 plates, drizzle with honey and sprinkle with sesame seeds.

*Beverage recommendation - hot green tea.

La Hacienda
Princess Resort
Lenard Rubin
Chef de Cuisine

Like the prodigal son, chef Lenny Rubin traveled afar, but now he is back home where he belongs.

Rubin originally made his mark as one of the Valley's first and best practioners of the art of Southwestern cuisine. His inspired creations earned him a devoted following and dozens of professional awards.

But the travel bug bit bigtime and Rubin headed off for the first of two cooking stints in Russia. From that base, he traveled widely and when he finally returned to the United States, he was accompanied by Russian-born wife Tatiana and son Sasha.

Heading up the kitchen at the prestigious La Hacienda is the perfect utilization for Rubin's talents. The turn-of-the-century inspired rancho deluxe is the only Mexican restaurant in the world to receive both the AAA Four Diamond and Mobil Four Star Award.

Authentic surroundings are enhanced by live music and the menu features such exciting dishes as roasted suckling pig and crab-stuffed sea bass.

❧ Kitchen tip from chef Rubin: "To avoid accidents, always keep your knives as sharp as possible."

La Hacienda: The Princess Resort, 7575 E. Princess Drive, Scottsdale. 585-4848
(Call for reservations and hours of business.)

Chicken Salad
with Roasted Pecans, Celery, Jicama and Dates

Salad

1 pound boneless, skinless chicken
   breasts cut in 1 inch cubes
juice of 1 lime
2 tablespoons olive oil
1 teaspoon cayenne pepper
salt and fresh ground pepper to taste
1 small onion, small dice
1 stalk celery, small dice

1/2 cup jicama, small dice
4 large dates, pitted and chopped
1/4 cup pecans, toasted, and
   coarsely chopped
2 tablespoons fresh cilantro,
   chopped
1/2 cup mayonnaise (more or
   less depending on taste)

Preheat oven to 350° In mixing bowl, toss chicken cubes with lime juice, olive oil, cayenne, salt and pepper. Place chicken in baking pan and bake 15 minutes. Let cool. Combine cooked chicken with the rest of the ingredients. Serve on chilled plates. Garnish with cilantro leaves if desired.

*Beverage recommendation - Horchata (a refreshing rice water and cinnamon drink, it can be found at Southwest supermarkets).

Shrimp and Roasted Corn Soup

Soup

1 cup corn kernels, fresh, frozen
   and thawed or canned and drained
2 teaspoons red chile powder
1 tablespoon corn oil
1 strip smoked bacon, diced small
1 tablespoon unsalted butter, room
   temperature, cut in pieces
2 tablespoons onion, diced small
2 tablespoons garlic, diced small
1 tablespoon tomato paste
1 tablespoon all-purpose flour
2 cups water

1 cup cream-style corn
1/4 pound rock shrimp, peeled
   and deveined
2 teaspoons red bell pepper,
   diced small
2 teaspoons green bell pepper,
   diced small
2 teaspoons cilantro, chopped
2 teaspoons green onion, chopped
2 tablespoons half and half
1/4 teaspoon fresh ground black pepper
salt to taste

Preheat oven to 400° Place corn kernels on baking sheet, sprinkle with cayenne and corn oil and bake about 15 minutes or until slightly browned. Meanwhile, in a sauce pot, cook bacon over medium heat until crisp. Add butter and stir until completely melted. Add onion and garlic and cook until softened. Add the tomato paste, stirring constantly for about 2 minutes. Add flour, stirring constantly about 1 minute. Slowly add water, whisking to break up any lumps. Bring to a boil, lower heat slightly and add cream style corn and roasted corn. Bring soup back to a boil and let simmer 10 minutes. Add the shrimp and vegetables and simmer a final 10 minutes, stir in half and half and adjust seasonings.

*Beverage recommendations - Margarita.

Grilled Tenderloin of Beef and Portobello Mushrooms with Poblano Cream

Entree

1 tablespoon corn oil
salt and fresh ground pepper to taste
8 3 1/2-ounce beef tenderloin filets

4 medium portobello mushrooms
1 cup poblano cream (see recipe below)

Poblano Cream

1 tablespoon corn oil
2 medium poblano chiles, seeded
   and chopped
1 clove garlic, chopped
1 tablespoon onion, finely chopped

1/4 cup dry white wine
1 1/4 cup heavy cream
2 tablespoons cilantro leaves
1 tablespoon unsalted butter
salt and fresh ground pepper to taste

In sauce pan heat corn oil over medium heat. Add the chiles and saute for 2 minutes. Add the garlic and onions and saute another minute. Add the white wine, bring to a boil and reduce by half. Add the cream, reduce by half again. Place sauce, cilantro and butter in blender and liquefy. Strain and season to taste.

Assembly

Prepare barbeque. Brush beef and mushrooms with corn oil and season with salt and pepper. Place on grill. Rotate one time to create grill "crossmarks". Do the same on the other side. Cook beef to desired temperature. Mushrooms should cook another 5 minutes. Remove from grill. Drizzle about 2 tablespoons poblano cream sauce on each plate. Place mushroom in the middle with 2 beef filets on top of the mushroom, leaning against each other.

*Beverage recommendation - Sangria Mexicana.

Potato and Cheese Enchiladas

Entree

12 6-inch corn tortillas
1 cup corn oil
1 1/2 cups prepared red enchilada sauce

1 1/2 cups cilantro-corn mashed
   potatoes (see recipe below)
1/2 pound jack cheese, grated

Cilantro-corn Mashed Potatoes

3 medium baking potatoes,
   peeled and quartered
2 teaspoons unsalted butter
2 tablespoons heavy cream

2 tablespoons sour cream
4 tablespoons cilantro leaves, chopped
2 tablespoons corn kernels, cooked
salt and fresh ground pepper to taste

In a sauce pan, bring potatoes to a boil in salted water. Lower heat and cook until tender (about 25 minutes). Puree potatoes, add rest of ingredients and combine thoroughly. Adjust seasonings.

Assembly

Preheat oven to 350°. In a sauce pot, heat cooking oil to medium-high. Using tongs, dip a tortilla in hot oil for about 10 seconds. Repeat with 3 more tortillas, overlapping them on the bottom of a small baking dish. Brush with enchilada sauce, spread a 1 inch layer of mashed potatoes on top and sprinkle with cheese. Heat 4 more tortillas and layer on top with sauce, potatoes and cheese. Top second layer with the remaining 4 tortillas, sauce and cheese. Bake 20 minutes or until cheese is golden-brown.

*Beverage recommendation - Dark Mexican Beer (such as Modelo Negro).

La Tâche
World Bistro & Wine Bar
Gregg Lamer-*Managing Director*
Eric Strong-*Executive Chef*

Those who say there is nothing culinarily new under the sun, need to vist La Tâche, it is one of the freshest and most captivating restaurants in the country. The internationally-inspired menu offers something to please virtually every taste.

Chef de Cuisine Eric Strong credits his diverse background for enabling him to come up with the far-ranging menu. Strong blends influences from a stint in the Bahamas to the broad food culture of his native Florida as well as culinary school in Washington, D.C., the adopted home of multiple ethnic cuisines.

La Tâche is the rare dining establishment where equal attention has been given to wine and wine-food pairing. This reflects the expertise of managing director Gregg Lamer, a certified sommelier and former beverage director at The Phoenician. The fold-over menu that immediately identifies what wines work with which food selections is one of Lamers innovations.

It is an exceptionally attractive restaurant as well, elegant yet comfortably casual. In keeping with the theme, wines and wine memorabilia from around the world provide the decorative elements.

❦ A tip from Chef Strong - "Cover leftover grated or diced fresh ginger with sherry and store in glass jar. It will keep indefinitely in the refrigerator."

La Tâche: 4175 Goldwater Blvd., Scottsdale.
946-0377
(Call for reservations and hours of business.)

Pepita-Crusted Crabcakes with Chipolte Aioli

Appetizer

1/2 cup lump crab meat
2 eggs
1/4 cup mayonnaise
2 tablespoons lime juice
1/4 cup breadcrumbs
1 tablespoon cilantro, chopped

1 teaspoon chile spice (see recipe below)
pepitas mix (1 cup toasted, chopped pepitas mixed
    with 1 cup breadcrumbs)
2 tablespoons olive oil
chipotle aioli (see recipe below)

Chile Spice

2 tablespoons red chile powder   2 tablespoons cayenne pepper   2 tablespoons cumin

Combine thoroughly. Store in glass container.

Chipotle Aioli

1/3 cup sour cream
1/3 cup mayonnaise
2 tablespoons lime juice
2 tablespoons cilantro leaves, chopped

2 garlic cloves, roasted and pureed
4 tablespoons chipotle peppers, pureed (available
    in Mexican food section of most supermarkets)
1 teaspoon chile spice (see recipe above)
salt to taste

In mixing bowl, combine all ingredients and mix well.

Assembly

Pick through crabmeat removing all shells. Whip eggs, mayonnaise and lime juice together. Fold in breadcrumbs, cilantro and chile spice and blend. Combine with crabmeat, Divide into four patties, pressing patties into pepita mixture to coat evenly. Heat olive oil in a saute pan and cook crab cakes until golden brown on each side. Place crab cakes on heated plate and dollop with chipotle aioli.

*Beverage recommendation - Gregg suggests a light, crisp wine such as Marc Bredif Vouvray, Loire Valley or Pinot Gris King Estate, Oregon.

Sauteed Scallop Salad with Baby Greens and Citrus Vinaigrette

Salad

The salad may be "dressed up" by using leaves of bibb lettuce, radicchio cups or Belgian endive as a cup or base.

3 cups mixed greens (preferably organic)
citrus vinaigrette (see recipe below)
salt and pepper to taste
8 orange segments
1 tablespoon total lemon, lime
    and orange zest

16 red pepper curls
16 large scallops
1/4 cup olive oil
toasted sesame seeds for garnish

Vinaigrette

1/2 cup salad oil
1/2 teaspoon sesame oil
1/4 cup rice vinegar
2 tablespoons orange juice

2 tablespoons lime juice
2 tablespoons lemon juice
1 garlic clove

1/4 teaspoon fresh ginger,
    peeled and grated
salt and pepper to taste

Combine all ingredients in a blender or food processor. Blend 30 seconds. Pour into a non-metal container and allow to sit in refrigerator overnight before using.

Assembly

Combine greens, vinaigrette, salt and pepper, zest and pepper curls, toss well. Heat olive oil in a skillet until very hot. Quickly sear scallops until golden brown and just set, Season with salt and pepper. Divide greens mixture on 4 plates. Top with orange segments and sesame seeds. Slice scallops and arrange around greens.

*Beverage recommendation - Gewurztraminer Trimbach, Alsace.

Provencal Pot Roast

Entree

3 lb top round roast
2 cups all purpose flour
1/2 cup olive oil
1/2 cup carrots, sliced
1/2 cup celery, sliced
1/2 cup onion, diced
8 garlic cloves

1 tablespoon thyme
1 tablespoon rosemary
1 tablespoon herbs de Provence
2 bay leaves
1 tablespoon salt
1 tablespoon fresh ground pepper
1 cup red wine

1/2 cup tomato paste
2 quarts beef stock
12 kalamata olives, pitted
4 roma tomatoes, quartered
garlic mashed potatoes
    (see recipe below)

Preheat oven to 350 F. Season beef with salt and pepper, dredge with flour and set aside. Heat a heavy pot, large enough to accomodate all ingredients. Add olive oil, heat and sear meat on all sides until very brown. Add carrots, celery, onions and garlic cloves. Saute until tender. Add thyme, rosemary, herbs de Provence, salt and pepper. Deglaze pot with red wine and stir in tomato paste. Add stock and simmer for 5 minutes until paste is dissolved. Add olives and tomatoes, cover pot and place in the oven for 2 hours. Check if meat is fork tender, if not bake an additional 30 minutes. (Be careful when removing cover.) Serve with garlic mashed potatoes.

Garlic Mashed Potatoes

4 potatoes (preferably Yukon Gold)
2 tablespoons olive oil
3 tablespoons chopped garlic

1 cup heavy cream
4 ounces butter, cubed
salt and pepper to taste

Place potatoes in a large pot & cover with cold water. Boil until soft, approximately 30 minutes. Heat oil in sauté pan, add garlic & brown lightly. Remove from heat. Heat cream in saucepan until boiling. Keep warm. Whip potatoes gradually adding garlic oil, cream & butter. Be careful not to overmix. Season with salt & pepper.

*Beverage recommendation - any California Zinfandel

Woked 5-Spice Beef and Rice Noodles with Sweet Chile Sauce

Entree

1 pound beef tips, marinated overnight in a mixture of 2 cups salad oil, 1/4 cup cornstarch and 2 - 3 tablespoons fresh ginger, peeled and sliced

3/4 cup peanut oil
1 head bok choy, sliced
2 carrots, julienned
1/2 cup shiitake mushrooms, sliced
1/2 cup fresh bamboo shoots
4 green onions, sliced
4 cloves garlic, minced

1 gallon water
1 pound rice noodles
sweet chile sauce (see recipe below)
2 tablespoons sesame oil
1 tablespoon sesame seeds, toasted
1/2 cup fried wontons

Sweet Chile Sauce

1/2 cup sweet chile sauce (Lee Kum Kee
    brand available at Oriental markets)
1/4 cup hoisin sauce
1 tablespoon oyster sauce
1 teaspoon 5 spice powder
1 tablespoon sesame oil
1 teaspoon fresh ginger, peeled and minced

1 teaspoon garlic, minced
1/4 teaspoon Szechuan peppercorns,
    finely ground
1 tablespoon chile garlic sauce
    (such as Sriracha Brand)

Combine all ingredients in a bowl. Mix well and allow to sit for 1 hour before using.

Assembly

Preheat wok for 3 - 5 minutes. Add peanut oil and beef. Cook beef to medium. Pour off excess oil. Add next seven ingredients and continue to move wok so food does not stick. Meanwhile bring water to a boil and add noodles for about 30 seconds or until they begin to separate. Remove noodles and carefully add to wok. Add sweet chile sauce and sesame oil to wok, toss vigorously. (Add 2 tablespoons boiling water to wok if mixture becomes too thick.) Divide among 4 plates. Garnish with sesame seeds and fried wontons.

*Beverage recommendation - George Duboeuf Beaujolais-Village or, if you prefer white, Wild Horse Pinot Blanc.

Manuel's
Mexican Restaurant
Alice Salazar and Family
Owners

Manuel's is a family restaurant in the truest sense of the word. Owned and operated by the Salazar family since 1964, the popular eateries are also a favorite stop for literally thousands of Valley families craving their weekly Mexican food "fix".

The original restaurant on 32nd and Indian School is still doing gang-buster business and now there are seven others spread from Glendale to Tempe. The high quality of the food is exactly the same as it was when Manuel and Alice Salazar first opened the doors.

Everyone seems to have a favorite dish, be it the standard Sonoran options or house specialties such as seafood enchiladas, Hawaian pork tacos and Mexico City Chicken. Manuel's margaritas are a local legend.

The Salazars children; John, David, Cindy Garcia and Patricia Romero are integral to Manuel's remarkable expansion. All have worked in the business since they were children. And, with 12 grand-children and two great-grandchildren coming up, it looks as if these family favorite restaurants are in for the long run.

🐝 A kitchen tip from David Salazar -"When green chiles are in season, fire up the grill and roast a bunch. After sweating, peeling and seeding, they can be frozen and enjoyed all year."

Manuel's:

1111 W. Bell Rd., Phoenix. 993-8778
12801 N. Cave Creek Rd., Phoenix. 971-3680
2820 E. Indian School Rd., Phoenix. 957-7540
3162 E. Indian School Rd., Phoenix. 956-1120
5509 N. 7th St., Phoenix 274-6426
1123 W. Broadway, Rd., Tempe. 968-4437
2350 E. Southern Ave., Tempe. 897-0025
5670 W. Peoria, Glendale. 979-3500
(Call for reservations and hours of business.)

Cheese Crisp with Fresh Green Chile and Green Onions

Appetizer

Manuel's is known for their classic cheese crisp. Here is the technique.

1 large flour tortilla
1/4 cup monterey jack cheese, grated
1/2 cup cheddar cheese, grated
fresh roasted green chile strips (see kitchen tip)
2 green onions, chopped
hot sauce or salsa of your choice

Preheat oven to 375.° Pierce the tortilla in several places with a toothpick or skewer. Place in oven on rack until it just starts to crisp. Remove and top with cheese. Put back in oven until cheese melts and bubbles being careful not to burn tortilla. Remove from oven, arrange chile strips and green onion on top. Cut into eighths and serve immediately with hot sauce or salsa on the side.

*Beverage recommendation-a jalapeno margarita (just a dash of jalapeno Tabasco sauce).

Albondigas Soup

Entree

With warm tortillas and salad, this hearty soup makes a meal.

3 quarts beef broth
1 large yellow onion, diced
1 1/2 cups celery sliced
1 cup carrots, sliced
1 10-ounce can diced tomatoes, with juice

1 cup fresh roasted and diced
 green chiles or 2 4-ounce cans
2 cloves garlic, minced
salt and pepper to taste

Put all ingredients in a large stockpot and cook over medium heat until vegetables are tender (about 45 minutes). Meanwhile, prepare meatballs.

Meatballs
1 1/4 pound ground beef
2 1/2 tablespoons raw rice
3 tablespoons flour
1 egg
1 teaspoon oregano (crush between your palms to release flavor)
1 clove garlic, minced
pinch cumin
salt and pepper to taste

In mixing bowl, combine all ingredients, mixing well. Roll meat into balls (about a heaping tablespoon of meat mixture each). Refrigerate briefly to set up. Add to soup the last 20 minutes of cooking time. Garnish bowls of albondigas with sprigs of fresh cilantro.

*Beverage recommendation - Corona beer.

Baja Dorado Fish Tacos

Entree

4 6-ounce mahi mahi filets
8 6-inch flour tortillas
marinade (see recipe below)
chorizo spice (Jesse Martinez Brand
    available on racks in some supermarkets)

seasoned salt (such as Lawry's)
prepared tartar sauce (adding a teaspoon
    of chopped green chiles gives a south-of-
    the-border flavor)
2 cups shredded cabbage

Combine cabbage with about 2 tablespoons of tartar sauce and set aside.

Marinade

1 cup corn oil
1/4 cup orange juice
1/4 cup lime juice

1 teaspoon chorizo spice
seasoned salt and pepper to taste

Combine ingredients and mix well.

Assembly

Pour marinade over fish and sprinkle with spice and salt to taste. Refrigerate 4 hours. Prepare barbecue grill. Place fish on grill skin side down. Brush with marinade at least twice before turning (about 2 - 3 minutes). Turn fish, pull off skin, repeat brushing with marinade. Cook another 1 or 2 minutes. Heat flour tortillas on grill until warm and flexible. Cut fish into quarter inch strips and divide between tortillas. Serve with cabbage and tartar sauce mixture.

*Beverage recommendation - sangria or iced lemonade with mint.

Skillet Apple Pie a la Mode

Dessert

This is a delicious "quicky" when you're in a hurry. The butter rum sauce stores well.
1 9-inch apple pie (from a bakery, frozen and baked or, if you feel ambitious, made from scratch)
Butter Rum Sauce (see recipe below)
vanilla ice cream

Sauce

1 teaspoon water
2 tablespoons unsalted butter
2 tablespoons sugar
2 tablespoons Karo dark corn syrup

2 tablespoons Karo Light corn syrup
1 teaspoon Myer's rum
1/2 teaspoon rum extract
1 teaspoon vanilla extract

In saucepan, combine water, 1 tablespoon butter and sugar. Bring to a boil. Add syrups to pan, bring to a boil again and lower to a simmer. Simmer 10 minutes. Add rum extract, vanilla extract and remaining tablespoon of butter and turn off heat. Let cool for 1 hour. Stir again.

Assembly

Preheat oven to 350.° Place heavy 10 inch skillet in oven and heat. Carefully remove pie from baking pan and place in hot skillet. Pour 1/2 cup butter rum sauce over and around pie and place in oven. Remove when heated through and sauce is bubbling. Cut pie into wedges, place on plates with scoop of ice cream on top.

*Beverage recommendation - Meyer's rum and coffee.

Marilyn's
First Mexican Restaurant
The Kobey Family

Marilyn's First Mexican Restaurant was first in more ways than one. With no previous restaurant experience, Marilyn and Cy Kobey found themselves with an instant success on their hands. The festively decorated restaurant has been packed with enthusiastic customers from the day it opened.

Not content to rest on her laurels, Marilyn broke new Mexican food ground by developing South-of-the-border recipes that are not only flavorful, but also health-oriented. This is the home of the original and much-duplicated spinach enchilada. New additions to the menu include glazed spit roasted chicken and the "serape wraps", succulent fillings tucked into handmade flour tortillas.

Fire-eaters know a secret about Marilyn's. The restaurant features one of the spiciest and best specialty hot sauces in town. This is also Celebration Central for hundreds of Valley families who choose Marilyn's as THE place to celebrate birthdays and other occasions.

The entire Kobey family is involved in the restaurant, and with their help Marilyn's latest venture is pre-prepared Mexican treats which are available at A.J.'s.

Marilyn's: 12631 N. Tatum Blvd., Phoenix.
953-2121
(Call for reservations and hours of business.)

Fiesta Salad

Salad

1 large head iceberg lettuce, shredded
1 large red pepper, julienned
1 large yellow pepper, julienned
2 avocados, sliced
1 medium onion, finely chopped
1 medium jalapeno, finely chopped
4 medium tomatoes, halved, cored and sliced
1/2 cup black beans, drained
1/2 cup corn kernals, cooked
2 cups tortilla strips (Marilyn's brand is available at A.J.'s
1/2 cup crumbled ranchero cheese (available at Southwest supermarket or substitute monterey jack)

Toss first 9 ingredients together in a large bowl, top with tortilla strips and cheese. Serve with your favorite dressing or salsa.

*Beverage recommendation - fruit flavored iced tea.

Spinach Enchiladas

Entree

2 1/2 cups monterey jack cheese, shredded
1/2 pound fresh spinach, chopped
1/2 cup white onion, diced

8 medium flour tortillas
enchilada sauce (see recipe below)

Enchilada Sauce

1 tablespoon butter
1/2 cup white onions, diced
1 1/2 cups half and half
1 1/2 cups 2% milk
1 1/4 teaspoons salt
1/2 teaspoon white pepper
1 teaspoon granulated chicken boullion

1/3 teaspoon dill
2 tablespoons butter or margarine
2 tablespoons flour
3/4 cup monterey jack cheese, shredded
1 1/2 cups sour cream
1 cup spinach, cooked, thoroughly
    drained and chopped

In saute pan, melt butter over medium heat. Saute onions until soft. In sauce pot, bring half and half and milk to a boil. Add onion, salt and pepper, dill and boullion to milk mixture. Stir. In small bowl combine flour and butter and add to milk mixture, combining thoroughly. Take off heat and allow to cool about 15 minutes. Fold in cheese, sour cream and spinach.

Assembly

Preheat oven to 350° In a medium bowl combine cheese, spinach and onions. Lay out tortillas and spoon 1/8th of the cheese mixture in the center of each and roll. Place in baking dish, seam down. Top with about a cup of enchilada sauce (any leftovers may be refrigerated and warmed later as a chip dip). Bake about 35 - 40 minutes or until cheese melts and top is golden.

*Beverage recommendation - Margaritas.

Tortilla Soup

Soup

1 quart water
2 tablespoons granulated chicken
   boullion
1/2 cup white onion, diced
1/2 cup green onion, chopped
1 1/2 pounds fresh green chiles,
   stemmed, seeded and sliced
1 tablespoon garlic, minced
1 cup carrots, diced
1 cup celery, finely chopped
2 cups tomatoes, peeled, seeded
   and chopped

1/2 cup tomato puree
1 3/4 teaspoons oregano
1 1/2 teaspoons cumin
1/4 teaspoon black pepper
salt to taste
2 tablespoons cilantro, finely chopped
1 cup jalapeno jack cheese, shredded
2 cups tortilla strips
1 medium avocado, cubed
cilantro sprigs for garnish (optional)

Put water and boullion in large sauce pot and bring to a boil. Add onions, green chiles, garlic, carrots, celery, tomatoes and tomato puree and lower heat. Cook until vegetables are soft, about 1 hour. Add spices and cilantro and stir well. Preheat broiler. Ladle soup into 4 ovenproof bowls. Top each with tortillas and cheese and melt in broiler. Top with avocado and cilantro sprigs and serve.

*Beverage recommendation - Corona beer with lime.

Vegi-ladas

Entree

2 tablespoons canola oil
1 pound potatoes, peeled, par-boiled
   and diced
1/2 medium white onion, diced
1/2 cup red and green bell peppers, diced

1/2 cup broccoli florets
1/2 cup corn kernels (fresh or frozen)
1/2 cup mushrooms, sliced
8 flour tortillas
enchilada sauce (see recipe below)

Enchilada Sauce

1 tablespoon canola oil
2 tablespoons white onion, diced
1 teaspoon garlic, minced
1 cup tomatoes, diced
1/2 cup zucchini, diced
1/2 cup mushrooms, chopped
1/2 cup corn kernels (fresh or frozen)

2 tablespoons chopped green chiles
   (canned are fine)
1 tablespoon tomato puree
1 teaspoon cilantro, chopped
1 teaspoon parsley, chopped
1 1/4 cups water
salt and pepper to taste

In large saucepan heat oil. Saute onion and garlic until soft. Add tomatoes and cook 5 minutes. Add zucchini, mushrooms, corn, green chiles, tomato puree, cilantro, parsley, water and seasonings. Cook over medium heat about 20 minutes. Slowly add flour and water mixture and cook additional 5 - 10 minutes stirring constantly until mixture thickens. Set aside.

Assembly

Preheat oven to 350° Heat canola oil in saucepan and saute potatoes and onion until onions soften. Add peppers and cook 2 minutes. Add broccoli, corn and mushrooms and cook until all veggies are al dente. Lay out tortillas and spoon 1/8 veggie mixture into the center of each. Roll and place seam down in baking pan. Top with about 1 cup of sauce and bake about 20 minutes.(leftover sauce can be refrigerated or frozen.)

*Beverage recommendation - Sangria.

Michelina's

Ristorante Costa Campagnia
Michelina Disibio

Chef-Owner

One of Manhattan's hottest restaurants is Le Madri, featuring "Mama-style" Italian cooking. New York has nothing on Phoenix. To the great delight of her many fans, Michelina Disibio has been doing the same thing here for almost a dozen years. Appropriately, she credits her own mama for passing on her cooking skills. Michelina's specialty is seafood, reflecting the coastal area south of Naples where she was born. Her menu is rich with options such as crispy calamari, linguini with clam sauce, and pasta with smoked salmon in a delicate cream sauce.

Michelina's personality comes through not only in her very personal style of cooking, but also in the charm of the cozy, warmly lit restaurant. Masses of fresh flowers are a signature and the three lovely and evocative paintings hanging on the walls depict her hometown of Gesualdo and herself, as a girl, with her mother.

The homey quality of the restaurant is also enhanced by a staff of three; Mary, John and Brad, who have been with Michelina virtually from the time she opened. They are as much "family" as Maddalena, Michelina's two year old granddaughter who can often be found in the kitchen keeping grandma company. It is Michelina's fondest hope, that someday Maddalena takes over the restaurant from her.

When not in the kitchen, the two "M's" relax by gardening together. And to recharge her batteries, Michelina hikes the Phoenix mountain preserves.

Michelina's: 3241 East Shea Blvd., Phoenix
996-8977
(Call for reservations and hours of business.)

Oysters Michelina

Appetizer

8 medium-sized fresh oysters in shell

Filling
1 1/2 cups fresh spinach, chopped
1 egg
1/2 tablespoon fresh garlic, chopped

1/4 cup grated parmesan cheese
1/2 cup grated mozzarella cheese

In a small bowl combine all ingredients.

Sauce
1 1/2 cup heavy cream
1/3 cup bay shrimp
1 teaspoon fresh parsley, chopped
1 tablespoon butter

1/4 teaspoon fresh garlic, chopped
1/4 cup grated parmesan cheese
paprika

Combine all ingredients except paprika.

Clean oysters well and open shell. Divide filling between each oyster and stuff. Place oysters in a saute pan and add sauce. Sprinkle with paprika and cook over medium heat about 7-8 minutes. Sauce will thicken. Serve warm. (Oysters and filling may be prepared a day ahead and cooked in sauce when needed.)

*Beverage recommendation - Italian Chardonnay.

Red Snapper with Clams and Mussels Over Linguine

Entree

Begin by cleaning the fish filets and checking for small bones, usually along one side, which can be removed with a small pliers. Then clean the clams and mussels to remove sand and other items from exterior of shells.

4 6-ounce red snapper filets
12 greenlip mussels
12 little neck clams
2 teaspoons fresh garlic, chopped
1/4 cup olive oil
1/2 cup white wine
6 cups fresh tomatoes, diced
  (canned or a combination of both is fine)

1 tablespoon fresh parsley, chopped
1 tablespoon fresh basil, chopped
1/2 teaspoon dried oregano
  (or 1 tablespoon fresh)
1 teaspoon red chiles, crushed (optional)
salt and pepper to taste
1 pound linguine cooked al dente

In a large skillet saute garlic in oil until golden. Add fish, mussels, clams and white wine. Add tomatoes and seasonings on top.
Cook over medium heat approximately 15- 20 minutes (a little underdone is preferable to over-cooked). The clams and mussels should be open and sauce thickened slightly. Arrange over cooked pasta on individual plates. Garnish with fresh basil leaves.

*Beverage recommendation - an Italian Pinot Grigio, a light red wine is also acceptable.

Mostaccioli with Broccoli and Sundried Tomatoes

Entree

Michelina says you can be creative with this dish. Keep it vegetarian or add some meat or chicken, You may even want to include more vegetables,

1 teaspoon fresh garlic, chopped
4 tablespoons olive oil
3 cups chicken broth
1/4 cup sundried tomatoes, chopped
1 teaspoon fresh basil, chopped
pinch red chiles, crushed (optional)
salt and pepper to taste

1 1/2 pounds broccoli flowerettes
(slightly steamed)
1 pound pasta (mostaccioli or penne),
cooked al dente
Parmigiana cheese, grated (to taste)

In a saucepan, sautee garlic in olive oil until golden. Add chicken broth, tomatoes and seasonings. Bring to a boil and cook 3 - 5 minutes. Add broccoli and cook another 5 - 6 minutes. Serve over cooked pasta. if desired, sprinkle Parmigiana cheese over pasta before adding sauce.

*Beverage recommendation - California Chardonnay.

Tiramisu

Dessert

There are several ways to serve this dessert. The most popular is in a wine glass by itself or perhaps, layered with espresso/marsala
soaked ladyfingers. Michelina likes to serve it as a filling and frosting for a sponge-style cake that is soaked with an espresso/marsala mix.

1 pound mascarpone cheese (Italian cream cheese available at specialty stores such as A.J.'s)
4 tablespoons sugar
1 small cup espresso, (approximately 1 ounce)
4 eggs, separated
4 tablespoons sweet marsala (Florio is a good brand)
shaved chocolate (optional)
ladyfingers or sponge cake (optional)

In a bowl, blend cheese, sugar, espresso and egg yolks with marsala until creamy. Set aside and keep cool. In another bowl, whip egg whites until firm. Fold the two together. Serve chilled.

(When layering with ladyfingers or sponge cake, make a mixture of 1/2 sweet marsala and 1/2 sweetened espresso in whatever quantity necessary to soak the cake. Alternate layers of soaked cake with Tiramisu. Top with Tiramisu and shaved chocolate.

*Beverage recommendation - Moscato.

Murphy's

Dale Villa
Executive Chef

Does anyone remember when Prescott was a sleepy little backwater, known primarily for cool summer weather and some even cooler Victorian homes? Good restaurants played a very small part in that equation. But in 1985, Paul Murphy changed everything when he opened his eponymous restaurant in historic downtown. From there everything seemed to boom for the town (it now even boasts a Costco). It certainly exploded for Murphy, who followed up his original success by opening the more casual Gurley St. Grill.

His original restaurant is in a structure that was built as a mercantile store in 1890. Sensitive renovation preserved the turn-of-the century flavor. It is a genuinely special place with high tin ceilings and old-time memorabilia. Even the original display cases have been preserved.

It isn't charm alone that has made this a national destination. Murphy prides himself on hiring the best, and that is certainly the case with Dave Villa.

Villa put himself through school by working every aspect of the restaurant business. After graduating from ASU with a degree in Electrical Engineering, he decided his real love was cooking. Spending time in kitchens as diverse as The Arizona Biltmore and Oscar Taylor, Villa now brings his unique fusion of Oriental, European and American Southwestern cuisines to the delighted patrons of Murphy's.

🍃 Kitchen tip from Dave Villa: "So often when people buy cookbooks, they are looking for familiar recipes or ones that sound appealing but not too tough to make. However, anything that turns out great results from a little effort. But always keep in mind, cooking should be fun and never be afraid to improvise."

Murphy's: 201 N. Cortez St., Prescott,
520-445-4044
(Call for reservations and hours of business.)

Fresh Fried Catfish

Appetizer

The growth of aquaculture in Arizona, Arkansas and Louisiana has made mild, fresh catfish readily available nationwide.

2 pounds catfish filets
buttermilk eggwash (see recipe below)

country breading (see recipe below)
Louisiana hot sauce (see recipe below)

Buttermilk Egg Wash

2 cups buttermilk

6 eggs beaten

Combine ingredients in a wide bowl, set aside.

Country Breading

2 cups cracker meal
2/3 cup wheat flour
2/3 cup corn meal

2/3 cup white flour
1 teaspoon garlic powder
1 tablespoon seasoning salt (such as Lawry's)

Combine ingredients, set aside.

Lousiana Hot Sauce

1 12-ounce bottle Durkee's or Red Devil hot sauce   3 tablespoons butter, melted

Combine ingredients. Set aside and keep warm.

Assembly

Cut catfish into 3/4" wide lengthwise strips. Dip each piece in eggwash, draining excess. Toss 3-4 pieces in breading until full coated. When all catfish is breaded, heat enough shortening to cover fish in heavy skillet & fry fish 7-10 minutes. Remove & drain on paper towels. Serve with side of hot sauce & slice of lemon.

*Beverage recommendation - Margarita.

Grilled Vegetable Salad

Salad

This combination of marinated, grilled vegetables, fresh greens, tart vinaigrette and feta cheese makes this salad both unique and healthful.

1 red onion, cut in squares (make sure
   all veggie squares are the same size)
1 red bell pepper, cut in squares
1 green bell pepper, cut in squares
1 zucchini, cut in squares
1 yellow squash, cut in squares
12 white mushrooms

4 wooden skewers, soaked in water
   about 20 minutes
1/4 cup olive oil
2 cloves garlic, minced
1 tablespoon fresh thyme (basil or
   parsley will do as well) minced
fresh cracked pepper to taste

4 cups mixed greens
1/2 cup red onion, julienned
1/2 cup carrots, julienned
1 cup jicama, julienned

champagne vinaigrette (see recipe below)
8 tablespoons crumbled feta cheese
8 tablespoons pepitas (can be obtained at
   Trader Joe's and Hispanic markets)
8 tomato wedges (garnish)

Vinaigrette

1/2 passion fruit syrup (or your
   favorite fruit concentrate)
1/3 cup champagne vinegar
2 tablespoons red wine vinegar

1 teaspoon shallot or red onion, chopped fine
2 tablespoons fresh cilantro leaves, chopped
1/2 cup light oil (canola, soybean or
   sunflower are best)

Place all ingredients in a bowl and whisk thoroughly. Rewhisk before use.

Assembly

Prepare barbecue. Toss veggies in olive oil and seasoning and alternate on skewers, beginning and ending with mushrooms. Grill until tender. In large bowl toss greens, onion, carrot and jicama with dressing to coat. Divide between 4 chilled plates. Sprinkle 2 tablespoons cheese and 2 tablespoons pepitas over each. Lay brochette atop salad and garnish with tomato wedges.

*Beverage recommendation - Murphy's Chardonnay (Markham Vineyards).

Herb Crusted Tournedos of Beef with Shiitake and Portobello Mushroom Ragout

Entree

4 8-ounce filet mignons
herb garlic rub (see recipe below)

garlic and herb crouton rounds
(see recipe below)

2 shallots, finely diced
1 1/2 pounds shiitake mushrooms, stems removed and julienned
1 1/2 pounds portobello mushrooms, stems removed and julienned
1/2 cup cabernet
1 tablespoon beef stock or consomme
cornstarch slurry (1 tablespoon each water and corn starch)

Cut steaks in half crosswise to make 2 tournedos each. Rub steaks generously with herb mix. In a heavy skillet, heat a little olive oil and saute tournedos to desired temperature. Set aside. To the hot skillet, add shallots and saute until transparent. Add both kinds of mushrooms and saute until soft. Add cabernet and reduce by 3/4. Add stock and reduce by 3/4 or until there is just enough liquid to hold the mushrooms together. Thicken with corn starch slurry (Consistency should be quite thick.)

Herb Garlic Rub

1 tablespoon thyme
1 tablespoon oregano
1/2 teaspoon basil
1 cup garlic, chopped

1 tablespoon cilantro leaves, chopped
1/2 teaspoon tomato paste
1/3 cup olive oil

In a small bowl, combine first 6 ingredients, add enough oil to moisten herbs & bind them together. Set aside.

(continued on page 152)

Jamaican Barbecue Pork Tenderloin with Mango Sour Cherry Compote

Entree

1 3-pound pork tenderloin
Jamaican barbecue sauce (see recipe below)

mango sour cherry compote
(see recipe below)

Jamaican Barbecue Sauce

1 cup honey
1/2 cup orange juice
1/2 cup pineapple juice
1/4 cup roasted garlic cloves,
chopped coarsely

1/4 cup Neera's Hot Jamaican Jerk Spice
(available at Cinnabar Specialty Foods in Prescott)
corn starch slurry (3 tablespoons each
corn starch and water)

Mix all ingredients in a saucepan and bring to a boil. Thicken with corn starch slurry to desired consistency.

Preheat oven to 300° Trim silver skin & excess fat from pork with a sharp knife. Tie the loin 5 times with butchers twine to help hold its shape. Brush with Jamaican barbeque sauce & place in oven for about 45 minutes or until internal temperature reaches 145° & let rest about 20 minutes. (Keep in mind the temperature will rise some 15 degrees while pork rests, so if you like it at 160° you'll be there.) While meat is cooking prepare compote.

Mango Sour Cherry Compote

2 ripe mangos, peeled and diced
1 cup dried sour cherries
1/4 cup sugar
1/2 teaspoon ginger powder

Combine all ingredients throroughly to dissolve sugar.

Assembly

Slice pork on the bias into 12 medallions. Place 3 on each plate "smiley face" fashion. Add compote around bottom of smile with half on plate and half on pork.

*Beverage recommendation - Murphy's Prescott Red Lager.

Old Town Tortilla Factory

Patrick Hughes
Chef-Owner
Cesareo Sebastian III
Sous Chef

Popular restaurants and cultural consciousness don't often go hand-in-hand, but they do at Old Town Tortilla Factory. The dynamic duo of chefs Patrick Hughes and Chase Sebastian is committed to preserving and interpreting Native American and Mexican culinary traditions. And, they do it in such a delicious way the restaurant is beginning to attain national prominence.

Nor does it hurt that this is one of the prettiest places in town. Surrounded by lush greenery, it has a charming patio and cozy, separate bar and lounge known as the Tequillaria. The interior of the restaurant itself is a subdued, non-cliched Southwestern-style, done in soft tones of creamy peach and sky-blue.

The menu clearly reflects the two Arizona-born chefs' vision, featuring signature dishes such as Navajo tacos, pescado Veracruzana and chicken empanadas. The "Tortilla Factory" part of the name is reflected in Hughes outstanding flavored tortillas which are fresh-made on the premises daily.

When they aren't working or traveling and researching their subject, the two chefs take similar paths. Both love the outdoors; Hughes is a mountain climber, Sebastian enjoys fishing in the mountains.

🍃 Kitchen tips from chefs Patrick and Chase: "Always wear gloves when handling chiles, so you don't rub oil in your eyes or on your skin.
Use kosher salt because it is not as strong as iodized. To keep from crying when cutting an onion, have someone else do it!"

Old Town Tortilla Factory: 6910 E. Main Street, Scottsdale
945-4567
(Call for reservations and hours of business.)

Smoked Corn & Sunflower Sprout Soup

Soup

Almost all Southwest Indian tribes smoke corn. The original idea was to preserve the corn, which will last for months. It has a very distinct flavor and gives a rich, deep complexity to recipes such as this soup. You don't need a smoker, just a barbecue grill with a simple modification.

6 ears smoked corn
2 tablespoons olive oil
1 cup celery, chopped
1 cup carrots, chopped
1/2 cup onions, chopped
1 tablespoon garlic, minced

1 gallon chicken stock
1 1/2 inch cinnamon stick
1/4 cup fresh oregano, chopped
kosher or sea salt and fresh cracked pepper to taste
sunflower sprouts for garnish (available at A.J.'S)

To smoke the corn, place husked ears in a smoker and smoke at 150° for 4 hours. If using a barbecue grill, start a wood fire and let burn about 20 minutes. Cover so the fire goes out, place corn in the barbecue, recover and smoke until corn is a dark brown color. In a heavy-bottomed sauce pan, heat olive oil and saute celery, carrots, onion and garlic until translucent, about 10 minutes. Remove corn from cob, place in pot and continue to cook for an additional 3 minutes. Add stock and seasonings and simmer for 30 minutes. Remove from heat, discard cinnamon stick. Garnish each bowl with sunflower sprouts.

*Beverage recommendation -Ferrari Carano Fume Blanc.

Tinga Poblana

Entree

In Puebla, Tinga Poblana is served as a stew, a filling for sandwiches or a stuffing for empanadas. This version is meant to be served as a stew with fresh corn tortillas or bread. You may also make this with chicken, beef or just vegetables, but remember, without chipotle peppers, it is no longer Tinga.

1 pound pork shoulder, trimmed and
    cut into 2 inch cubes
1/4 teaspoon dried thyme
1/4 teaspoon dried marjoram
2 teaspoons kosher or sea salt
2 bay leaves
3 new potatoes, diced
1 tablespoon olive oil
3/4 cup chorizo, casing removed
1 medium onion, diced

1 1/2 pounds roma tomatoes, roasted and peeled
    (Tomatoes can be roasted either in the oven at 325° or
on the grill until skin blisters. Sweat in a bag & remove skins.)
1/4 teaspoon dried marjoram
2 chipotle chiles, canned in adobo sauce,
    chopped (available in the Mexican food section of
    most supermarkets)
4 teaspoons of adobo sauce (from above)
1 teaspoon maple syrup

In a heavy saucepan bring a quart of water to a boil. Add the pork, skimming away foam that rises to the top. Add thyme, marjoram, salt and bay leaves. Simmer until tender about 1 hour. Remove meat and let cool. Strain leftover broth and retain about 1 cup. When meat is cool enough to handle, break into smaller pieces and set aside. Meanwhile, boil potatoes in salted water until fork tender. In a saucepan, brown the chorizo in olive oil. Remove chorizo from the pan but reserve drippings. In the same pan, brown together the pork and onions. Then add the tomatoes (crush with your hands), reserved pork broth and potatoes and simmer 5 - 10 minutes. Add marjoram, chipotles, adobo sauce and maple syrup and simmer 5 more minutes. Garnish with avocado slices and queso fresco or any soft farmer-style cheese.

*Beverage recommendation - Sangria.

Pollo Tampiqueno

Entree

This recipe comes from the Tampiqueno region of Northern Mexico. At first look there seems to be a lot involved here, but it's actually easy to produce and all ingredients are readily available.

1 pound tomatillos, simmered (always available at Southwest supermarkets)
6 whole jalapeno peppers
1 teaspoon cumin
1/2 teaspoon black pepper
2 teaspoons oregano
1 teaspoon salt
4 garlic cloves
1/2 teaspoon cinnamon
1/2 cup onion, coarsely chopped

1 cup slivered, blanched almonds
1/4 cup dry-roasted peanuts
1/2 cup pepitas (available at Trader Joe's and Southwest supermarket)
2 pieces white bread
1/2 cup orange juice
4 cups chicken broth
3 tablepoons pork lard or vegetable oil
2 fryers, about 3 pounds each, cut into pieces
flour for dredging

Combine all ingredients in blender except broth, oil and chicken and process well. Add some chicken broth if it is too thick to blend. In a skillet, heat 2 tablespoons of the lard or oil until hot or until a small amount of sauce added to the pot sizzles. Add sauce to pot and fry 5 minutes. Remove from heat and transfer into another container. Dredge chicken in seasoned flour. Heat remaining tablespoon of oil in same skillet, add chicken and cook until golden brown. Remove chicken from pan and drain off excess oil. Return chicken to pan, add sauce and rest of broth and cover. Cook over low heat for 20 minutes. Remove cover and cook 5 minutes longer. Season to taste. Serve with white rice.

*Beverage recommendation - Modelo Especial.

Peach Cobbler with Pecan & Cornmeal Crust

Dessert

When harvest season arrives, Native Americans celebrate and give thanks for Mother Nature's gifts. This recipe captures the sweetness and richness the season offers.

7 ripe peaches, peeled and sliced
3 tablespoons brandy
1/4 cup sugar

2 tablespoons cornstarch dissolved in 3 tablespoons water
pinch cinnamon

Topping

1/2 cup chopped pecans
1/2 cup brown sugar
1/4 cup yellow corn meal

1/4 teaspoon salt
2 sticks unsalted butter

Preheat oven to 350° Crush 2 of the peaches and add along with the brandy to a saucepan. Heat just to a boil and burn alcohol off using a long fireplace match. Be careful as brandy flames quickly. Reduce heat and cook until flame goes out. At this point stir in cornstarch mixture and cook until liquid is clear. Allow to cool completely. Prepare topping by combining all ingredients in a bowl, coarsely cutting butter in with hands but being sure not to overmix. The butter should be BB sized. Set aside.
Mix together sliced peaches with sauce. Place peach mixture in a 10 inch tart pan or 4 individual oven-proof ramekins and distribute topping over all. Bake 20 - 25 minutes or until filling starts to bubble. Serve with vanilla ice cream and fresh berries.

*Beverage recommendation - Patron XO Cafe coffee liqueur made with tequila.

Pane e Vino
Scott Ekenberg, Phil Pagnotta and Vincent Amendola
Owners

Pane e Vino is a new addition to the bustling North Scottsdale/Carefree area. The restaurant is spacious yet cozy with comfortable booths and warm lighting as well as a charming patio for clement weather dining. A separate lounge area features live entertainment and many customers choose to end the evening there with espresso and a drink.

The centerpiece of Pane e Vino is an exhibition kitchen with chefs busily preparing regional Italian specialties. Some of the menu highlights are snails with artichokes and hazelnuts, gnocchi in a mascarpone cheese sauce and spaghetti frutti di mare.

Pane e Vino's serving staff is smoothly professional and dedicated to making every meal an occasion.

Between them, Pane e Vino owners Scott Ekenberg, Phil Pagnotta and Vincent Amendola have many years of culinary experience and the restaurant is the culmination. They especially pride themselves on having put together a wine list that will please everyone from the casual diner to the most serious oenophile.

Pane e Vino: 8900 E. Pinnacle Peak Rd. Suite D-1, Scottsdale. 473-7900
(Call for reservations and hours of business.)

Arselle e Peoci Umido
(Stewed Mussels and Clams)

Appetizer

Serve this hearty appetizer with slices of toasted ciabatta bread.

1 pound clams
1 pound mussels
3 tablespoons olive oil
small white onion, minced
2 tablespoons parsley, minced
1/2 cup dry white wine
3 large tomatoes, diced
fresh grouund pepper to taste
parsley (optional garnish)

Scrub clams and mussels. In large saucepan over medium heat saute onion and parsley in olive oil. Add wine and shellfish and as they begin to open, add tomatoes and pepper. When fully opened and tomatoes have softened a bit, distribute shellfish between 4 dishes and garnish with parsley if desired.

*Beverage recommendation - Lolonis Fume Blanc 1996.

Insalata Rustica

Salad

2 heads chicory
2 large potatoes, peeled, boiled and sliced
4 small tomatoes, cut in wedges
4 hardboiled eggs
1 teaspoon mustard
1 cup heavy cream
1 tablespoon vinegar
fresh ground pepper and salt to taste
3 tablespoons olive oil

Wash and dry chicory and arrange leaves in a salad bowl. Place potatoes and tomato wedges on top. Chop the egg whites and sprinkle on top. Pass yolks through a sieve into a small mixing bowl and whisk with cream, vinegar, salt, pepper and oil. Pour over salad and serve.

*Beverage recommendation - Beringer Private Reserve Chardonnay 1995.

Medaglion di Vitello alla Panna (Veal Medallions in Cream Sauce)

Entree

1 pound veal tenderloin
3 tablespoons butter
1/4 pound pancetta (available at A.J.'s)
1/4 pound prosciutto (available at A.J.'s and Trader Joe's)
1 cup flour
1 cup veal stock or half chicken and half beef broth
1/2 cup white wine
3/4 cup heavy cream
salt and pepper to taste

Cut veal into 8 two ounce medallions. Cut a pocket into each medallion and stuff in a piece of pancetta and piece of prosciutto.
Dredge medallions in flour. Heat butter in a large skillet and saute the veal. When it is brown on both sides, add stock and wine to pan. Cook 5 - 7 minutes. Remove veal to a serving platter. Add cream and salt and pepper to pan and reduce, stirring, until thickened. Pour sauce over veal and serve.

*Beverage recommendation - Prinsi Barbaresco 1990.

Calamari con Piselli all' Anconetana (Squid and Peas Anconda Style)

Entree

Serve with linguinie or rice.
2 pounds squid, cleaned and cut into rings
4 tablespoons olive oil
1 stalk celery
10 basil leaves
1 cup white wine
1 pound peas, fresh or frozen
salt and pepper to taste
parsley (optional garnish)

Heat olive oil in a large skillet and saute the squid along with the celery and basil. Add the wine and simmer about 45 minutes or until calamari is tender (add more wine or fish stock as needed). Meanwhile, steam peas and saute in a little olive oil. Before serving combine peas with calamari and salt and pepper to taste.

*Beverage recommendation - Sanford Barrel Select Pinot Noir 1994.

Quill Creek Cafe
Grayhawk Golf Club
Jeff Storcz
Executive Chef

It's a toss-up which is the most spectacular aspect of Quill Creek Cafe, the unparalled view of the golf course with desert and mountain vistas beyond, or Jeff Storcz' scintillating culinary creations. Bottom-line, the two combined make this restaurant a genuine destination.

The Southwestern-accented interior is a pleasant blend of casualness and formality with lots of warm-toned woods and a bustling demonstration kitchen. In clement weather, the ramada-style patio, complete with wood-burning fireplace, is a prime dining site. Hints of the West are reflected in the menu, too, but Storcz doesn't limit himself and there are other culinary influences to be found as well.

The menu runs the gamut from highly sophisticated; featuring dishes such as apple-walnut crusted pork chops in red wine sauce and crispy prawn and basil wonton salad, to the very straightforward campfire steak sandwich.

Storcz kick-started his career at the age of 15 when he spent a summer working in the kitchen at Greer's White Mountain Lodge. After going through a rigorous apprenticeship program he put in time both at The Princess Resort and Ritz-Carlton.

Talk about being in the right place at the right time, Storcz favorite sport is, yes, golf.

🐾 A cooking tip from chef Storcz -"Simpler is always more effective."

Quill Creek Cafe: 8620 E. Thompson Peak Parkway, Scottsdale
502-1700
(Call for reservations and hours of business.)

Coconut Banana Cornbread

Appetizer

1 cup yellow cornmeal
1 cup all-purpose flour
1 tablespoon sugar
1 tablespoon baking powder
1 1/4 teaspoon ground allspice

1/2 teaspoon salt
1 egg, beaten
1 cup mashed bananas (about 2, very ripe)
1/4 cup milk
1/4 cup vegetable oil
1/2 cup sweetened flaked coconut

Preheat oven to 350° F. Grease an 8 inch square pan (or 2 6x3 loaf pans, set aside. In medium bowl, combine first 6 ingredients, forming a well. In another medium bowl, combine egg, bananas, milk and oil. Add milk mixture to dry mixture all at once and stir just to combine. Stir in coconut. Pour into pan and bake about 25 minutes until cake tester inserted in middle comes out clean. Cut into slices or squares and serve hot with butter.

*Beverage recommendation - Grand Marnier.

Crispy Prawn and Basil Wonton Salad
with Papaya Fruit Salsa and Citrus Ginger Dressing

Entree

citrus ginger dressing (see recipe below)
papaya salsa (see recipe below)

prawn wontons (see recipe below)
4 cups mixed greens

Citrus Ginger Dressing

1 cup green onion, chopped
1/2 cup chopped cilantro
1/4 cup fresh ginger, grated
3 cloves garlic, minced
1/2 cup sesame oil
1 1/2 cup soy sauce

1/4 cup rice wine vinegar
1/4 tablespoon fresh ground black pepper
1/4 cup brown sugar
3/4 cup orange juice
1/4 cup sesame seeds

Place all ingredients in a medium bowl and whisk together. Set aside making sure to blend again before tossing with greens.

Papaya Salsa

2 papayas, peeled, seeded and diced
1/4 cup red onion, diced
1/4 cup cilantro, chopped
1/2 teaspoon garlic, minced

1 medium tomato, diced
1 teaspoon jalapeno, seeded and diced
1 tablespoon fresh lime juice

Combine all ingredients in a medium bowl and mix well. Set aside.

Prawn Wontons

12 U-15 shrimp (if using smaller ones, use more),
    peeled, butterflied and deveined
1/2 cup Boursin cheese
1/2 cup cream cheese

1/2 cup fresh basil, chopped
24 3-inch wonton skins
1 cup sesame seeds

In a medium bowl combine cheeses. Add basil and mix well. Stuff cream cheese mix into each shrimp and set aside. Dip 12 wonton skins in water and lay out on work surface. Place a shrimp on each skin. Dip 12 more skins in water and place on top. Crimp edges together for a tight fit. Sprinkle with sesame seeds pushing into skin.

Assembly

Deep fry wontons until shrimp are cooked & wontons golden brown, about 2 -3 minutes. Drain. Meanwhile toss greens with dressing & divide among 4 plates. Place 3 wontons on top of greens & sprinkle with salsa.

*Beverage recommendation - Pouilly Fuisse.

Stuffed Chicken in Phyllo with Asparagus and Tomatoes

Entree

4 8-ounce skinless, boneless chicken breasts
vegetable oil
salt and pepper to taste
2 cups water
1 cup Boursin cheese

1 egg
8 asparagus stalks, diced
2 tomatoes, seeded and diced
12 sheets phyllo dough
6 ounces melted butter

Heat saute pan, add oil to cover bottom. Sprinkle chicken with salt and pepper. Sear chicken on both sides until about 3/4 cooked. Set aside to cool. In medium pot, boil water. Cook asparagus until semi-soft. Cool. Set aside. In mixing bowl, add cheese, asparagus, tomatoes and one egg. Mix thoroughly. Preheat oven to 350° F. Slice chicken breasts in half lengthwise. Divide cheese into 4 portions. Place 1/4 cheese mixture on 4 chicken halves topping with the other half. Set aside. Lay out one sheet phyllo dough and brush all over with melted butter. Lay two more sheets over the first repeating the buttering process. Lay chicken in center of triple sheet and wrap. Repeat with other breasts. Brush outside of each packet and bake 20 - 25 minutes or until phyllo is golden-brown.

*Beverage recommendation - Gundlach Bundschu Cabernet Sauvignon.

Indian Pudding with Vanilla Bean Sauce

Dessert

2 tablespoons plus butter
1/2 cup raisins
3/4 cup brown sugar
3/4 cup yellow corn meal
1 cup pumpkin puree
4 eggs

8 ounces half and half
zest from 1/2 lemon
1/2 teaspoon cinnamon
1/4 teaspoon nutmeg
vanilla bean sauce (see recipe below)
fresh berries

Preheat oven to 300 F. Butter four 3 inch foil round tins and sprinkle bottom with raisins. Melt rest of butter. In medium bowl, combine brown sugar, cornmeal and pumpkin. Add butter and let set 1 hour. Combine eggs, half and half, lemon zest and spices and add to cornmeal mix. Pour into tins, Place puddings in 3 inch deep pan filled halfway with water and cover with foil. Bake for 1 - 1 1/2 hour or until cake tester comes out clean. Serve warm or cold with vanilla bean sauce and berry garnish.

Vanilla Bean Sauce

1 vanilla bean
6 egg yolks
8 ounces sugar
8 ounces milk

Slice vanilla bean and scrape out inside. Pour milk in a medium saucepan, add vanilla scrapings and bring to a simmer. Combine sugar and egg yolks in a mixing bowl. Add half of milk to yolk mixture, folding together. Add this mixture back into other half of milk and whip constantly over low heat until thickened. Remove from heat and place pan in ice bath until chilled, stirring constantly.

*Beverage recommendation - Baileys Irish Cream Liqueur and coffee.

Remington's
Richard Sederholt
Executive Chef

Tucked inside a greenery draped, free-standing territorial style building just south of Scottsdale Plaza Resort, Remington's is one of the prettiest restaurants in town. The interior is rancho deluxe, warm and welcoming, with gleaming tile floors, substantial furniture, specimen plants, working fireplaces and an impressionistically lit, painted blue sky ceiling.

Yes, the restaurant's name derives from the famous cowboy artist Fredric Remington and there are several of his bronze sculptures on display. Just outside, the lushly planted patio with a view of Camelback mountain is a justly popular lunch spot. In the evening, there is live entertainment in the adjacent lounge.

But it is more than the seductive surroundings and excellent serving staff that draws the diners. Rick Sederholt, executive chef of the resort since 1989, has crafted a highly original menu for the restaurant. The style is regional American with an emphasis on bold flavors and imaginative meldings of ingredients. Creations such as cashew chicken fritters and shrimp and andouille pasta have put Remington's in the upper tier of Valley dining establishments.

In addition to overseeing Remington's, The Garden Court Restaurant and the resort's banquet kichen, Sederholt is deeply involved in the community, participating in programs as diverse as the Cystic Fibrosis Summer Youth Camp and ZooFari.

Remington's: Scottsdale Plaza Resort, 7200 N. Scottsdale Rd., Scottsdale, 951-5101
(Call for reservations and hours of business.)

Pan-Seared Duck on a Rosemary Pancake with Wilted Greens and Dried Berry Relish

Appetizer

This dish won the 1997 Chef's Choice Award in the Scottsdale Culinary Festivals Mayor's Cup Appetizer Competition.

1 10-ounce boneless duck breast
kosher salt and fresh ground black pepper to taste
1 tablespoon virgin olive oil

2 cups assorted greens
dried berry relish (see recipe below)
4 rosemary pancakes (see recipe below)

Dried Berry Relish

1 cup assorted dried berries (strawberries,
　blueberries, cranberries)
1 orange, zest and juice only

1 ounce aged balsamic vinegar
1 ounce virgin olive oil
1 teaspoon fresh tarragon, chopped
kosher salt and fresh ground black pepper to taste

Place orange juice, zest, vinegar and oil in a saucepan and warm slightly over low heat about 2 minutes. pour the mixture over the berries and toss. Add the tarragon and season with salt and pepper. Let relish stand at room temperature for 45 minutes covered with plastic wrap. Stir frequently.

Pancakes

1/2 cup yellow cornmeal
1/4 cup all-purpose flour
1/2 teaspoon sugar

1/4 teaspoon kosher salt
1/4 teaspoon baking powder
1/4 teaspoon baking soda

1/2 cup buttermilk
1 tablespoon vegetable oil
1/2 teaspoon fresh rosemary, finely chopped

Mix the cornmeal, flour, sugar, salt, baking powder and baking soda together. In a small bowl, combine buttermilk, egg, oil and rosemary. Stir the buttermilk mixture into the cornmeal mixture until well-blended. The batter will be slightly lumpy. Lightly oil a skillet and place on medium heat. Pour the batter in silver dollar-sized pancakes. Cook until golden brown on both sides and reserve at room temperature on a plate and covered with plastic wrap.

Assembly

Preheat oven to 350°. Season the duck breast with salt & pepper on both sides. Place in ovenproof pan and roast for approx. 20 minutes or until medium. Remove from oven, let stand 3 minutes. Heat a skillet over medium heat until hot, place duck skin side down and brown until crispy (watch for excess smoke, lower heat if necessary). Remove and place on cutting board. Warm tablespoon of olive oil and toss with greens until wilted. Season with salt and pepper. Divide greens evenly on four plates. Place a pancake on each pile. Slice duck breast, divide equally and arrange on crepes. Place a tablespoon of relish on top of duck letting it flow over the sides. Garnish with a sprig of rosemary.

*Beverage recommendation - Willamette Valley, Oregon Pinot Noir.

Pan Seared Salmon with a Light Herb Horseradish Crust and Mango Vinaigrette

Entree

Serve with rice, risotto, a vegetable stirfry or salad.

4 7-ounce boneless salmon filets
2 tablespoons olive oil
salt and fresh ground pepper to taste

1/2 cup herb horseradish crumbs (see recipe below)
1 cup mango vinaigrette (see recipe below)

Herb Horseradish Crumbs

1/2 cup dried white breadcrumbs
1 tablespoon fresh grated or prepared horseradish

1 tablespoon chopped fresh herbs (basil, cilantro, etc.)
1 tablespoon olive oil
pinch salt and fresh ground pepper

Place all ingredients in a blender and puree until smooth. Season to taste. Reserve at room temperature.

Mango Vinaigrette

1 cup fresh mango, peeled and cubed
3 tablespoons rice wine vinegar

1 tablespoon sake (optional)
salt and fresh ground pepper to taste

Place all ingredients in a blender and puree until smooth. Season to taste and refrigerate.

Assembly

Preheat oven to 350 F. place a large pan over medium high heat. Season salmon with salt & pepper. Put oil in pan, then salmon. Sear until brown & turn (approx. 2 min. on each side). Remove from pan and place in oiled ovenproof pan. Bake salmon 10 minutes or until just barely done. Remove and generously coat with crumbs. Place back in oven an additional 2 - 3 minutes. Remove. Ladle vinaigrette on plates and place salmon on top.

*Beverage Recommendation - Grgrich Hills, Fume Blanc.

Mesquite Grilled Lamb Chops
with Thai Peanut Sauce and Kettle Chips

Appetizer

This can also be served as an entree with larger portions. The sauce goes with chicken as well as lamb and the chips you can eat any time.

12 rib lamb chops, preferably New Zealand
(have your butcher "french" them)
pinch salt and fresh ground pepper

1 cup Thai peanut sauce (see recipe below)
kettle chips (see recipe below)
1 tablespoon chopped mint (optional garnish)

Thai Peanut Sauce

3/4 cup chicken stock or broth
1/4 cup creamy peanut butter
1 tablespoon fresh ginger root, peeled and grated

1 teaspoon soy sauce, low sodium variety
pinch red pepper flakes (or more if you like it hot)
salt and fresh ground pepper
1 tablespoon cornstarch and water mixture

Place all the ingredients with the exception of cornstarch mix in a saucepot over medium heat. Simmer for several minutes until all ingredients are incorporated. The sauce should thicken enough to coat the back of a spoon. (If it needs thickening add a little of the corn starch mix.) Season to taste. Keep warm.

Kettle Chips

2 large potatoes, russet or Idaho
1 quart canola oil
salt, seasoned salt or Cajun spice

Preheat oil in a deep pot until 350° (test with a thermometer). Wash potatoes and slice paper thin. Place sliced potatoes in a colander and wash under hot running water for about 5 minutes. Then let stand in water another 5 minutes. Drain the potatoes and dry with paper towels. Fry the chips several at a time until golden brown and remove to drain. Season and keep warm.

Assembly

Prepare a barbecue grill. Season lamb with salt and pepper. Grill to desired temperature. Ladle sauce on plate and place chops on sauce. Garnish with chips and chopped mint.

*Beverage recommendation - a classic Bombay Sapphire Martini.

Scottsdale Mixed Grill

Entree

Serve this dish with grilled potatoes and vegetables or just a simple baked potato and salad. The barbeque glaze can also be served with different meats, chicken or grilled fish. Be creative with it.

4 4-ounce filet mignons
2 game sausages or Italian sausages
8 large shrimp, peeled and deveined

1 tablespoon olive oil
salt and fresh ground pepper to taste
2 cups roasted garlic barbecue glaze (see recipe below)

Roasted Garlic Barbecue Glaze

12 large cloves garlic, peeled
3 tablespoons olive oil
1/4 cup onion, finely diced
1/4 green pepper, finely diced
1/2 jalapeno, seeds removed and finely chopped
2 teaspoons barbecue seasoning
1 tablespoon liquid smoke seasoning

2 tablespoons brown sugar
1/4 cup orange juice
2 tablespoons molasses
1 teaspoon worcestershire sauce
1/2 cup tomato sauce
1 cup ketchup

Preheat oven to 350°. Coat the garlic cloves with a little olive oil and place in an oven proof pan. Roast garlic until brown and soft, about 15 - 20 minutes and reserve. Add remainder of olive oil to a saucepan. Bring to medium heat and saute the onion, peppers and jalapeno for about 5 minutes or until onion is transparent. Add the rest of the ingredients to the pot and stir until incorporated. Simmer for 15 minutes. Mash the roasted garlic and add to pot. Stir and keep warm.

Assembly

Prepare barbeque grill. Rub oil on the shrimp and season shrimp and filets with salt and pepper. Place sausage on grill first, followed by filets and finally the shrimp. This controls order of doneness. Cook sausage until cooked through (about 20 minutes), filet to desired temperature and shrimp very briefly until they turn pink and firm. Remove from grill. Place barbeque glaze on each plate. Slice sausages into 6 slices (three per person). Arrange meats and shrimp on plate. Serve rest of sauce on the side.

*Beverage Recommendation - Williaim Hill Reserve, Cabernet Sauvignon.

The Rose
Restaurant
Linda Rose
Chef-Owner

Linda Rose took a long and winding road to get to the top of the heap as owner of The Rose, Prescott's newest and hottest dining establishment.

Back in New York, she owned and operated a liquor store while her husband ran a popular restaurant. One fateful night, his chef quit, and Linda, a good home cook, stepped in. She remained for 12 years until she moved to Prescott.

There, she started as a line cook at Hassayampa Inn and eventually became the executive chef. In that position she helped make Hassayampa a must-stop on the Northern Arizona culinary trail. (During her free time, she completed a certification program with the American Culinary Federation). Now, she is blazing a trail of her own with The Rose, on historic Cortez Street.

Rose has completely redone the charming Victorian cottage, keeping it light and bright with shades of cream, rose (of course!) and green. Works of local artists line the walls.

Culinarily speaking, Rose is known for being very responsive to her customers. "Whether it is on the menu or not, if they want it and we have it, I'll make it." she says. To her fans delight, signature "Vealinda" is on the menu and so are the exotically flavored flans and delicate but intensely chocolate-y desserts she is known for.

❦ A kitchen tip from chef Rose: "To save time, prep ahead as much as possible."

The Rose: 234 S. Cortez, Prescott
520-777-8308
(Call for reservations and hours of business.)

Mixed Greens with Raspberry Vinaigrette

Salad

Experiment by adding chopped walnuts and diced apples to the greens in this recipe. By adding broiled or grilled chicken breast, you turn it into a meal.

4 cups mixed seasonal greens
1 1/3 tablespoons red onion, diced
2 2/3 cups raspberries, frozen
1/3 cup olive oil
1 tablespoon balsamic vinegar
1 2/3 tablespoons red wine vinegar
3/4 tablespoons basil

1 teaspoon black pepper
2 teaspoons salt
1/3 cup sugar
1 1/3 tablespoons lemon juice
couple shakes Tabasco sauce
1/3 cup olive oil

Combine all ingredients in a mixer and blend throughly. Refrigerate overnight to let flavors blend. Toss with greens to taste and serve on chilled plates. Any leftover dressing will keep indefinitely in the refrigerator.

*Beverage recommendation - White Zinfandel.

Angelhair Pasta with Tomato Fennel Sauce

Entree

This recipe shares the twin virtues of being quick to prepare and light, perfect for a summer mealtime.

1 bulb fresh fennel, stalk removed
4 tablespoons olive oil
3 cloves garlic, thinly sliced
1 tablespoon whole fennel seed
pinch cayenne pepper
pinch basil
1 tablespoon anisette or Pernod
1/4 cup white wine
1-1/2 cups crushed tomato, canned or fresh
2 tablespoons sundried tomato, rehydrated and julienned
1 pound angel hair pasta

Slice fennel bulb in half, continue to slice diagonally as thin as possible. Set aside. Heat olive oil in skillet and saute garlic until golden, add fennel and continue to saute until it softens. Add dry ingredients, then anisette. Add wine, both kinds tomatoes and simmer until blended about 15 minutes. While simmering sauce, cook angel hair in boiling salted water until al dente, drain and divide between 4 heated bowls. Top with sauce and serve immediately.

*Beverage recommendation - Chardonnay.

Pork Chops and Cherry Peppers

Entree

4 whole potatoes
1 tablespoon olive oil
1/2 inch thick pork chops
2 cups cherry peppers, seeded and sliced
1 1/3 cup beef stock
1/2 cup sherry wine
salt and pepper to taste

Preheat oven to 350° Parboil potatoes, cool and cut in 1/2 inch slices. Set aside. In medium skillet, heat oil and sear chops on both sides. Remove to baking dish, reserving skillet with juices. Bake pork chops 15 minutes or until desired temperature. Meanwhile place in skillet with reserved juices, potatoes, peppers, stock and sherry. Simmer until liquid is reduced by half. Place one chop on each heated plate and top with potato and pepper mixture. Serve immediately.

*Beverage recommendation - Chianti.

Chocolate Dream Brownies

Dessert

4 ounces unsweetened baking chocolate
2 cups sugar
4 ounces margarine
4 large eggs
1 teaspoon vanilla extract
1 teaspoon baking powder
1 1/4 cups all purpose flour, sifted
1/4 cup walnuts, crushed
1/4 cup frozen raspberries, defrosted and drained
1/4 cup chocolate chips

Preheat oven to 325°. Melt unsweetened chocolate in top of double boiler. In a large bowl, cream sugar and margarine until fluffy. Add eggs one at a time and beat until smooth. Add melted chocolate and blend well. Add vanilla and baking powder. Slowly add flour. Blend until smooth. Fold in walnuts, raspberries and chocolate chips. Coat 8 1/2 by 11 inch baking pan with margarine and dust with flour. Pour batter into pan and bake for 25 minutes. When cool dust with confectioners sugar and serve.

*Beverage recommendation - espresso and Chambord.

RoxSand
RoxSand Suarez Scocos
Chef-Owner

Very simply, RoxSand is restaurant royalty, one of the small handful of Valley chefs who have put Phoenix on the culinary map and whose fame has spread nationwide.

RoxSand's style of cuisine is a seamless blend of different culinary traditions honed over the course of owning five restaurants, as well as a wholesale bakery and catering company. Her present restaurant, a striking contemporary space, is a backdrop for food that explodes with color and flavor.

RoxSand is deeply involved in Chefs Collaborative 2000, an organization dedicated to using as much organic and locally grown produce as possible. She is also an executive committee member of the International Association of Women Chefs and Restaurateurs, an organization designed to promote the education and advancement of women in the restaurant industry.

RoxSand and her husband and partner Spyros have two young daughters.

RoxSand: 2594 E. Camelback Rd. (Biltmore Fashion Park), Phoenix
381-0444
(Call for reservations and hours of business.)

Okra and Sweet Corn Gumbo
with Buttered Squash Timbales

Soup

1/4 cup olive oil
1/2 cup onions, chopped
1 teaspoon salt
3/4 teaspoon white pepper
1/2 teaspoon cayenne pepper
1/4 teaspoon black pepper
3/4 teaspoons dry mustard
1/2 teaspoon dried thyme leaves
1/4 teaspoon dried basil leaves
1-2 bay leaves

1 teaspoon garlic, minced
1 stalk celery, chopped
1 tablespoon butter
1/8 cup flour
1/2 cup okra, cut crosswise in 1/4 inch slices
1/2 cup red bell pepper, julienned
1/2 cup sweet corn kernels (preferably fresh)
4 scallions trimmed and sliced
Italian parsley, chopped (garnish)

In large saucepan over medium heat saute onions in oil until translucent. Add salt, pepper and spices and mix. Add garlic and celery and saute until tender. Add butter and flour, cook until mixture forms a roux. Add okra, red bell pepper and corn, cooking together briefly. Add water. Bring to a boil then simmer for 45 minutes. Saute the scallions and add to the above. While soup is cooking prepare squash timbales.

Buttered Squash Timbales

1 whole spaghetti squash
1/2 pound butter, melted and browned

salt and pepper to taste

Place squash in pot of boiling water. Lower heat and simmer until it can be easily pierced with a fork. Once cool enough to handle, cut in half and remove seeds. Using a fork, gently remove the 'spaghetti' strands. Toss with browned butter and salt and pepper. Form into 3 ounce timbales or twirl into "nests". Place a timbale in center of soup plate and ladle gumbo around. Garnish with parsley if desired.

*Beverage recommendation - Sauvignon Blanc.

Heirloom Potato Strudel
with Shiitake Cabernet Sauce

Entree

This is a versatile dish that can be served as a vegetarian entree or as a hearty accompaniment to poultry or meat.

4 large Heirloom potatoes, peeled
   and thinly sliced
4 tablespoons olive oil
3/4 teaspoon fresh ground black pepper
1 1/2 teaspoon salt
4 tablespoons butter
1 1/2 large onion, diced

3 tablespoons parsley
3/4 cup ricotta cheese
2 eggs
16 sheets filo dough
3/4 cup butter, melted
shiitake cabernet sauce (see recipe below)

Heat olive oil in heavy skillet. Fry potatoes until brown and crispy. Add salt and pepper. Remove from pan. Heat butter and saute onions until translucent. Add to reserved potatoes. Pulse in food processor until coarsely mashed. Chill slightly. Once cool add parsley, ricotta and eggs and mix thoroughly. Preheat oven to 350°. Lay out filo sheets carefully, keeping those not in use covered with a damp cloth. Brush one with butter and lay second sheet over it. Put 1/2 cup potato mixture just below the center of the sheet and fold filo over to make triangular shape. Make 7 more pieces. Brush outside of each strudel with butter and place on a baking sheet. Bake about 20 - 30 minutes or until golden brown.

(continued on page 152)

Snapper with Herb Broth and Mushroom Mashed Potatoes

Entree

Herb Broth

2 tablespoons butter
1 1/2 teaspoon garlic
1 tablespoon shallots, chopped
2 1/4 cups chicken stock, reduced by half
1 tablespoon basil

1 tablespoon chervil
1 tablespoon thyme
3 tablespoons carrots, diced
3 tablespoons celery, diced
3 tablespoons red bell pepper, diced

In skillet melt 1 tablespoon butter over medium heat and sweat garlic and shallots. Add stock, bring to a boil. Lower heat to a simmer and reduce by a third. Add herbs and vegetables and remaining butter. Set aside.

Wild Mushroom and Yukon Gold Mashed Potatoes

1 3/4 pound Yukon Gold potatoes
1 tablespoon garlic, minced
1 cup cream

1/2 cup wild mushrooms
1 teaspoon thyme
1 cup vegetable stock

Place all ingredients in a heavy bottomed pot. Bring to boil and lower heat, cooking until potatoes are fork tender. Transfer to mixer or food processor and mash. (Do not overbeat or mixture will become glutinous). Keep warm.

(continued on page 152)

Warm Blueberry Tart with Ginger Ice Cream

Dessert

Tart Shell

1/2 cup sugar
1 teaspoon vanilla extract
1/2 teaspoon salt

4 egg yolks
1/2 cup unsalted butter
1 3/4 cups flour

Cream together sugar, vanilla, salt, yolks, butter and flour. Wrap dough in plastic wrap and chill. Roll dough, and cut to fit a 10 inch flan ring or pie pan.

Filling

2 eggs
5 tablespoons sugar
1/2 cup heavy cream
1 1/2 teaspoon melted butter

1/3 cup all purpose flour
grated zest of 1/2 orange
1 pint blueberries, washed and picked over

Whip eggs with sugar until white and foamy. Add cream, butter, flour and orange zest and combine thoroughly. Pack unbaked tart shell with blueberries and pour filling over all. Bake in 350° oven for 20 - 25 minutes. Serve warm with ginger ice cream.

Ginger Ice Cream

2 cups milk
1/4 cup fresh ginger, chopped

5 egg yolks
2/3 cup sugar
1 cup cream, whipped to hold a soft shape

Bring milk almost to a boil. Add ginger and infuse for one hour. Beat yolks with sugar until thick and light. Whisk in half of hot milk and whisk that mixture back into remaining milk. Heat gently, stirring constantly with a wooden spoon until slightly thickened. Strain and chill then place in ice cream freezer. When partially set, add the whipped cream and continue freezing.

*Beverage recommendation - coffee and brandy.

Squash Blossom

Hyatt Regency Scottsdale at Gainey Ranch
Anton Brunbauer
Executive Chef

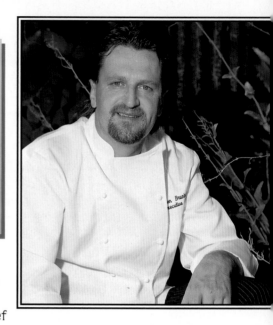

Squash Blossom is one of Hyatt Scottsdale's three outstanding restaurants under the direction of executive chef Anton Brunbauer. It is one of the few resort restaurants that is patronized as enthusiastically by locals as it is guests. And, for good reason. Spacious, airy and comfortable, Squash Blossom offers outstanding food with a distinct and memorable Southwestern twist.

Breakfast features such goodies as blue corn griddle cakes with berries or pinon nuts. At lunch and dinner, diners can go light with a crisp salad or choose from hearty options such as an adobo marinated steak.

Brunbauer, who comes from a long line of Austrian restaurateurs and innkeepers, apprenticed at the tender age of 15. Since then he has honed his skills in some of the finest hotels and restaurants in the world. He has been with Hyatt Scottsdale since 1986.

Married with two sons, Brunbauer balances numerous charitable and community activities with spending off-time on the slopes. He is widely known as a demon skier.

Squash Blossom: Hyatt Regency Scottsdale, 7500 E. Doubletree Ranch Rd., Scottsdale. 991-3388 (Call for hours of business.)

130

Gazpacho

Soup

2 medium cucumbers, peeled and
    coarsely chopped
5 medium ripe tomatoes, coarsely chopped
1 large onion, coarsely chopped
2 medium green bell peppers, stemmed,
    seeded and coarsely chopped
4 cups water

3 cups French bread, coarsely crumbled
1/2 cup olive oil
1/4 cup red wine vinegar
4 teaspoons salt
1 tablespoon garlic, chopped
1 tablespoon tomato paste
cumin to taste

Garnishes

1 cup onion, chopped
1 cup cucumber, chopped

1 cup bell pepper, chopped
1 cup croutons

In a deep bowl combine all ingredients except garnishes and mix thoroughly. Ladle mixture into blender, 2 or 3 cups at a time and blend for 1 minute at high speed. Pour puree into a bowl and chill well for 1 or 2 hours. Serve garnishes on the side.

*Beverage recommendation - Markham Vineyards Napa Valley Sauvignon Blanc.

Southwestern Shrimp Caesar

Entree Salad

Toasted olive bread is the ideal accompaniment to this hearty and flavorful salad.

20 16/20-size shrimp, peeled and deveined
shrimp marinade (see recipe below)
2 tbs olive oil to saute shrimp
Caesar dressing (see recipe below)
3 hearts of romaine lettuce, cores removed,
    washed in cold water and torn into 1 1/2 inch pieces

1 cup fresh corn kernels
2 medium tomatoes, cut in 1/2
    inch cubes
1/2 cup parmesan cheese, grated

Shrimp Marinade

1/4 cup olive oil
2 tablespoons soy sauce
2 tablespoons fresh oregano, chopped

2 tablespoons basil, chopped
1 tablespoon garlic, chopped

In medium bowl, combine marinade ingredients with shrimp tossing well. Cover and refrigerate one half hour, mixing occasionally. Saute shrimp in 2 tablespoons oil over medium heat until just pink and firm (do not overcook). Set aside.

Caesar dressing

1 cup mayonnaise
1/4 cup lemon juice
3 tablespoons soy sauce

2 tablespoons parmesan cheese, grated
2 teaspoons brown sugar
1/2 teaspoon cayenne pepper

Assembly

In deep bowl, toss romaine, corn, tomatoes and dressing to taste. Divide between 4 chilled plates, topping each with 4 or 5 sauteed shrimp. Garnish with grated parmesan.

*Beverage recommendation - Chardonnay.

Barbecued Pork and Eggplant Wrap
with Mixed Greens

Entree

marinade (see recipe below)
12 1 1/2-ounce pork loin portions (fat removed)
1 medium eggplant, sliced into
   12 quarter inch slices
3 medium carrots, peeled and julienned
1 medium jicama, peeled and julienned

1 medium cucumber, peeled, seeded
   and julienned
2 cups prepared barbecue sauce,
   warmed
4 12-inch jalapeno-cilantro flavored
   tortillas (available at A.J.'s)
mixed greens

Marinade

1/2 cup olive oil
1/2 cup prepared barbecue sauce
1/4 cup lemon juice

1 tablespoon garlic, chopped
1 tablespoon oregano, chopped
1 tablespoon basil, chopped

Assembly

In large bowl, combine marinade ingredients and mix thoroughly. Add pork and eggplant to mixture, cover and refrigerate one half hour, mixing occasionally. Grill over medium heat 3 - 4 minutes per side. Top warmed tortillas with 1/4 cup barbecue sauce, 3 pieces pork, 3 slices eggplant, carrots, jicama and cucumber. Roll each tortilla and cut into 3 slices. Place on plates with mixed greens.

Mixed Greens

1/2 cup olive oil
1/2 cup lemon juice
salt and pepper to taste
head Boston Bibb lettuce, cleaned
   and cut into bite-size pieces
1 medium red onion, thinly sliced

bunch red oak leaf lettuce, cleaned
   and cut into bite-size pieces
bunch Curly Endive, cleaned and cut
   into bite-size pieces
2 medium tomatoes, thinly sliced
16 kalamata olives

Whisk oil and lemon juice together until well-blended. Season to taste. In mixing bowl, toss lettuce and dressing. Arrange on 4 serving plates and top with onion, tomato and olives.

*Beverage recommendations - Pinot Noir.

Crème Brûlée

Dessert

1 vanilla bean, split lengthwise
1 quart heavy cream
10 egg yolks
3/4 cup granulated sugar

Preheat oven to 350 ° Scrape seeds out of vanilla bean and place in 2 quart saucepan with the cream. Bring to boil over moderate heat. In large mixing bowl whip yolks with sugar. Pour a steady stream of boiling cream into the yolk mixture, whipping constantly. Scrape off any foam and divide between 4 8-ounce ovenproof gratin dishes. Place on 18 x 13 sheetpan, add 1/2 inch very hot water and place in oven for 30 - 35 minutes. Remove from oven when 3/4ths set (tap sheet pan, custard should jiggle slightly). Cool on rack for 15 minutes. Refrigerate 6 hours or overnight. Prior to serving generously sprinkle brulee tops with sugar. Either with a hand torch (available at Williams-Sonoma) or directly under the broiler, melt and brown sugar on top of brulee's. Cool slightly before serving.

*Beverage recommendation - Steele dessert wine.

Steak & Sticks
Joey Bistro
Los Abrigados Resort
Scott Uehlein
Executive Chef

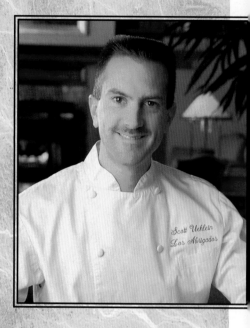

Set like a jewel in the fabled red rock country, Los Abrigados is one of the few resorts in the state that draws visitors all year round. In the winter, the luxurious resort has become known for its spectacular holiday light show. The rest of the year the place is packed thanks to an array of the finest amenities.

Among those amenities are two of the best restaurants in the area, Joey Bistro and Steaks & Sticks, both under the direction of chef Scott Uehlein. Joey Bistro features Southern Italian fare, Certified Angus beef is the draw at Steaks & Sticks. Both restaurants are noted for their superb selection of vintage wines.

New Jersey-born Uehlein is a graduate of top-drawer Culinary Institute of America, and his resume lists dozens of honors. He enjoys synthesizing regional ingredients into his creations as was evident in the menu he prepared at a recent James Beard House appearance which included chipotle prawns with epazote-oregano oil and smoky herbed beef tenderloin with onion jalapeno relish.

Uehlein is married with two small children and when not at the range, enjoys time at home with his family.

❦ A kitchen tip from Chef Uehlein: "When grilling, remove fish or meat just prior to its finished cooking. Cover and let sit until it reaches proper doneness. This prevents drying or overcooking."

Joey Bistro and Steaks & Sticks: Los Abrigados Resort, 160 Portal Lane, Sedona.
520-282-1777
(Call for reservations and hours of business.)

Spicy Beef Salad

Salad

Here is a salad that can easily work as an entree. It is the chef's interpretation of a favorite Thai dish with Southwestern flavors added.

1 pound flank steak
chile rub (see recipe below)

dressing (see recipe below)
4 cups assorted seasonal greens

Chile Rub

1 tablespoon crushed red chile peppers
1 tablespoon garlic powder
1 tablespoon red chile powder

1 tablespoon onion powder
1 tablespoon curry powder
1 teaspoon ground coriander

Mix spices together and rub into flank steak. Prepare barbecue grill and cook chile-rubbed steak about 10 minutes on each side until beef is done to desired temperature. Refrigerate and prepare dressing.

Dressing

1/4 cup chile oil
1/4 cup rice vinegar
2 teaspoons fresh ginger, minced
2 teaspoons fresh garlic, minced
1 bunch green onions, cleaned
   and sliced
1 bunch cilantro, roughly chopped

3 jalapeno peppers, stemmed and
   seeded, finely chopped
1/4 cup soy sauce
3 tablespoons lime juice
1 red onion, sliced
1 each red and yellow bell peppers,
   seeded and sliced

In a bowl, combine chile oil, vinegar, ginger, garlic, green onion, cilantro, jalapenos, soy and lime juice and whisk vigorously. Add onions and peppers. Slice slightly cool meat in strips and toss with dressing. Divide the greens between 4 chilled plates and top each with an equal amount of beef and dressing. Serve immediately.

*Beverage recommendation - Gewurztraminer or Reisling from Alsace.

Veal Chops with Peach Rosemary Salsa

Entree

Try this one at the height of peach season when they are plenty ripe. Any leftover salsa will work with grilled chicken as well.

4 6-ounce veal chops
peach rosemary salsa

Salsa

2 cups fresh peaches, peeled, seeded
   and diced (about 3 large peaches)
1/4 cup red pepper, finely diced
1/4 cup yellow pepper, finely diced
1/4 cup green onions, cleaned and chopped
2 tablespoons fresh ginger, chopped

1 tablespoon fresh garlic, chopped
2 tablespoons fresh rosemary, chopped
juice of 2 limes
1 jalapeno, stemmed, seeded and minced
   (optional but adds that extra kick)
salt and pepper to taste

Mix all ingredients and let stand about 30 minutes while preparing grill and cooking veal to desired doneness. Top each cooked chop with salsa.

*Beverage recommendation - Sauvignon Blanc.

Panzarotti Joey Bistro

Appetizer

This is a combination of a fried mozzarella stick and a potato croquette.

1 1/2 cups cooked potato,
   peeled and diced
1 egg yolk
3 tablespoons parmesan cheese

1 tablespoon fresh basil, chopped
24 1/4-inch cubes mozzarella cheese

Breading
1 cup flour
2 eggs, beaten
2 cups bread crumbs
1 tablespoon dried basil
2 teaspoons garlic powder

1 teaspoon crushed red chiles
1 teaspoon salt
3 cups oil for frying
2 cups mixed greens

In a bowl add egg yolk, basil and parmesan to cooled potatoes and mash together until smooth. Form into 8 1 1/2-inch long croquettes. Press 3 mozzarella cubes into each and reform around it. Bread each croquette in flour eggwash and breadcrumb mix. Heat oil until temperature reaches 350° and fry panzarotti until golden brown, about 4 minutes. Drain. Arrange greens on each of 4 chilled plates. Place 2 panzarotti atop and drizzle each with a tablespoon of vinegar.

*Beverage recommendation - Chianti.

Pork Tenderloin with Roasted Tomatoes and Fennel Celeriac Slaw

Entree

This dish is as flavorful as it is calorie conscious.

2 12-ounce pork tenderloins, trimmed
1/2 cup olive oil

3 garlic cloves, minced
2 ripe tomatoes, cut in half

Combine oil and garlic and marinate tenderloins about 30 minutes. Meanwhile, prepare slaw.

Slaw
juice of 3 limes
1 tablespoon sugar plus 1 teaspoon
salt and pepper to taste

1 bulb fresh fennel, thinly sliced (save tops)
1 medium-sized bulb of celeriac, julienned
6 leaves fresh basil, cut in thin ribbons

In a bowl, combine lime juice, sugar, salt and pepper. Add fennel, celeriac and basil and toss. Set aside.

Assembly
Preheat oven to 400° In ovenproof skillet, over high heat sear marinated tenderloins until brown. Add tomatoes and place in oven for about 20 minutes, turning both tomatoes and pork occasionally, until internal temperature of meat reaches 165° Remove from oven. Arrange 4 plates with slaw. Slice tenderloins and place on slaw. If desired, drizzle with a little olive oil and decorate plate with reserved fennel leaves.

*Beverage recommendation - Pinot Grigio.

Tarbell's
Mark Tarbell
Chef-Owner

Overnight stars are not just a Hollywood phenomenon. It happened in the valley two years ago when Tarbell's opened and the restaurant became an instant, blazing success. But, like other, similar stories, a lot of hard work and talent came first.

Owner Mark Tarbell, formerly food and beverage manager at The Boulders resort, has a thorough culinary grounding and encyclopedic knowledge of wines. That, combined with great personal charm and a clear vision of exactly what he wanted in a restaurant has really paid off.

It is a sophisicated venue, sleek and clean-lined but with a comfortably relaxed feel. The cuisine could be described the same way. Tarbell's philosophy is to use the very best ingredients and prepare them with simplicity and integrity. The result is remarkably straightforward, full-flavored food.

Creations such as smoked rock shrimp with plum tomato relish, soft shelled crab with an Oriental inspired sauce, one of the best steak and fries around, and exceptional desserts have become instant legends. Of course, the wine list lives up to the food, and the staff is admirably prepared to help with stellar selections.

A kitchen tip from Mark Tarbell - "Keep it simple, keep it fresh."

Tarbell's: 3213 E. Camelback Rd., Phoenix.
955-8100
(Call for reservations and hours of business.)

A Wedge of Iceberg with Cool Blue Dressing

Salad

1 firm head iceberg lettuce
Cool Blue Dressing

Dressing

1/3 pound blue cheese
1/4 cup parmesan or romano cheese,
 finely grated
2 teaspoons extra virgin olive oil
juice of 2 - 3 lemons (about 1 cup)

1 - 3 garlic cloves, minced (according to taste)
1/2 cup non-fat mayonnaise
1 splash worcestershire sauce
1 splash low sodium soy sauce
1 teaspoon Dijon mustard

Whisk together all ingredients except oil and cheese until smooth. Slowly add oil and cheese to mixture. On chilled, dark-colored salad plates, pool dressing. Cut lettuce in quarters and place on dressing cut side up. Dive in!

*Beverage recommendation - Pinot Grigio Alois Lageder 1995

Lamb Tenderloin
with Spring Vegetables and Brown Rice

Entree

8 lamb tenderloins (about 4 ounces each)
2 red bell peppers, halved lengthwise,
 seeds and membrane removed
1 tablespoon butter
2 shallot bulbs, minced
1 cup brown rice
1 1/2 cups water

1/3 cup tomatoes, seeded, cored, chopped
3 tablespoons parsley, chopped
salt to taste
lemon juice to taste
olive oil to taste
1/2 pound asparagus, peeled
lemon yogurt mint sauce (see recipe below)

Lemon Yogurt Mint Sauce

1 bunch fresh mint, finely chopped
1/2 cup white wine vinegar
juice of 1 lemon

3/4 cup low fat yogurt
1 teaspoon extra virgin olive oil

Blend ingredients together well. Set aside.

Prepare barbecue. Grill lamb 5 - 10 minutes to desired temperature. At same time, grill pepper halves which have been brushed with a little oil until browned slightly. Set aside. Melt butter in a sauce pan and cook shallots until tender. Add brown rice and water. Bring to a boil, reduce heat to simmer. Cover and cook 20 minutes or until water is absorbed. Remove from heat. When cool, add tomatoes, parsley, salt, lemon juice and olive oil to taste. Steam asparagus for 5 minutes. Toss with salt, lemon juice and olive oil to taste.

Assembly

Slice lamb on the diagonal (3 slices per tenderloin). Divide rice between 4 heated plates, heaping it in the center of each. Fan 6 slices of lamb over rice. Cut peppers in 4 slices each. Arrange 2 slices of pepper and 2 asparagus spears at top half of plate. On bottom half, ladle Yogurt sauce in a half circle at base of rice.

*Beverage recommendation - Pride Mountain Merlot, Napa 1995

Grilled Pork Tenderloin with Smoked Four Onion Relish and Sweet Potato Cakes

Entree

1 1/2 pound pork tenderloin
1 pound fresh spinach leaves, whole
olive oil and lemon juice to taste

Four Onion Relish (recipe below)
Salsa Verde (see recipe below)
Sweet Potato Cakes (see recipe below)

Relish

4 green onions   1 white onion   1 red onion   2 cloves garlic

Preheat oven to 400° Trim, peel and slice all ingredients. Place onions on a sheet pan and bake until caramelized about 12 minutes. Set aside.

Salsa Verde

4 fresh tomatillos (always available
   at Southwest supermarket)
1/3 bunch flat leaf parsley
1 serrano chile
1 clove garlic

2 tablespoons lime juice
1 tablespoon water
1 tablespoon canola oil
salt to taste

Puree all ingredients. Set aside.

Sweet Potato Cakes

3 raw sweet potatoes (organic, if possible), grated
1 poblano chile, charred, peeled and diced
1 Anaheim chile, charred, peeled and diced

4 - 5 ounces pancetta or bacon,
   diced and fried until crisp
1 tablespoon olive oil or clarified butter

In medium bowl, mix ingredients together. Heat oil or butter in a skillet. Form 4 pancakes from the potato mixture and sear on each side. Set aside.

Assembly

Prepare barbecue. Grill tenderloin until desired temperature. Set aside. In hot skillet, saute spinach with oil and lemon to taste. Place a potato cake on each of 4 plates, Top with spinach, then onion relish. Cut tenderloins on the diagonal into 12 slices each. Fan 6 slices next to pancake. Ladle salsa in a crescent around pork.

*Beverage recommendation - A light, slightly chilled Pinot Noir such as Hamilton Russell Vineyards Pinot Noir, South Africa.

Rustic Strawberry Shortcake with Fresh Whipped Cream

Dessert

2 pints fresh strawberries, stemmed and rinsed
2 cups whipped cream
2 teaspoons sugar
2 cups flour

2 teaspoons baking powder
pinch salt
1 1/2 cups heavy cream
4 ounces butter, melted

Preheat oven to 400° In mixing bowl, combine dry ingredients. Add cream, mixing as little as possible. Chill dough slightly. Melt butter. Roll out dough to 3/4 inch thick and cut into 4 2-1/2 inch rounds. Dip rounds in butter, place on sheet pan and bake 15 to 18 minutes or until golden brown. Split shortcakes, arrange on plates and top with berries and cream.

*Beverage recommendation - Moscato d'Asti "Nivole" Michelle Chiarlo, 1995.

Tucchetti
Lettuce Entertain You Enterprises, Inc. *Owner*
Scott Harlig *General Manager*
Mike Dooher *Chef-Manager*

Dining at Tucchetti's is like being welcomed into the bosom of a big, happy Italian family. Just walking in the door causes spirits to soar. The decor is cozy and comfortable from the grapevine draped arbor overhead to the old-time photos on the wall and the homey red and white checkered coverings on the tables. Delectable odors waft through the air and the music of favorite crooners like Frank Sinatra and Dean Martin add to the sense of fun and festivity.

Tucchetti's staff prides themselves on providing complete satisfaction to every customer from the tiniest bambino to the most venerable Nana. The antipasti-salad bar is a favorite way to start the experience. Bountiful with fresh greens, ripe tomatoes, cheeses and all the trimmings as well as crocks of steaming minestrone, diners can do it their way, or ask one of the servers to dish it up for them.

All meals are accompanied by irresistible garlic bread and this is THE place to indulge in old favorite dishes, among them baked spaghetti, ravioli, stuffed shells and lasagne. Tucchetti features six chicken specialties and the thin crust pizzas have become a Valley legend. Portions are ultra-generous but savvy regulars know to save room for one of the luscious desserts.

Tucchetti is owned by world-famous Lettuce Entertain You restaurants. Based in Chicago, Lettuce is one of the major independent restaurant groups in the nation with more than 40 stores. Founder Rich Melman is legendary in the business for his innovation and sound business sense.

Tucchetti: 2135 E. Camelback Rd. (Town and Country Shopping Center), Phoenix. 957-0222
(Call for reservations and hours of business.)

Spinach-Artichoke Cheese Dip

Appetizer

Serve with thinly sliced garlic bread that has been lightly dusted with paprika and toasted.

Tip: Any leftover dip can be tossed with hot pasta for a great meal.

1 1/2 cups fresh spinach leaves
1 tablespoon olive oil
2 cloves garlic, crushed
4 ounces sun-dried tomatoes, rehydrated and chopped
4 ounces canned artichoke hearts, drained and chopped
4 ounces Asiago cheese, shredded
8 ounces cream cheese, at room temperature
scant 1/2 cup prepared Alfredo sauce (available in most grocery stores)

For topping:
1 ounce Parmesan, shredded

Preheat oven to 375° F. Heat olive oil in skillet, sautee garlic until golden. Add spinach and cook until soft. Allow to cool enough to handle, squeeze dry and chop. Combine Asiago, cream cheese and Alfredo sauce. Blend in sauteed spinach, tomatoes and artichokes. Place mixture in an ovenproof casserole. Top with Parmesan and bake about 5 minutes until cheese on top browns.

Chopped Chicken Salad

Salad

8 cups lettuce (mixture of your choice), finely chopped
1 cup tomatoes, diced
8 scallions, chopped
8 ounces cooked chicken breast, diced

1 pound cooked pasta (elbows, bowties or small shells)
8 ounces Danish blue cheese, crumbled
1 cup salad dressing (see recipe below)

Dressing

Makes about 1 quart, keeps well in the refrigerator
Tip: can also be used as a marinade for chicken and pork.

1 tablespoon Coleman's Dry mustard
1/2 cup sugar
1 tablespoon garlic, pureed
1/2 cup water
1/4 cup red wine vinegar
1/3 cup white vinegar

1 teaspoon salt
2 cups vegetable oil
1/2 cup mild olive oil
1 teaspoon dried oregano
1/2 teaspoon dried red chiles, crushed
1 teaspoon black pepper, ground

Combine mustard, sugar, garlic, water, red and white vinegar and salt in a blender or food processor. While it is running, slowly drizzle in the two oils. Add remaining ingredients and mix briefly. In a large bowl, toss vegetables, chicken, pasta, cheese and dressing.

Chicken Siciliano

Entree

12 ounces angel hair pasta
4 boneless, skinless chicken breasts, approximately 6 1/2 ounces, lightly pounded
flour to dredge
4 tablespoons vegetable oil
1 cup onions, thinly sliced
4 teaspoons extra virgin olive oil
4 garlic cloves, thinly sliced
1/2 cup fresh basil leaves, julienned

1/2 cup sun-dried tomatoes, rehydrated, drained and julienned
16 pitted whole black olives (substitute imported kalamata olives for a more intense flavor)
1/2 cup dry white wine
2 cups chicken stock
chopped parsley (optional)

Cook pasta until al dente and set aside. Dredge chicken breasts in flour. Heat vegetable oil in a heavy skillet and saute chicken until both sides are lightly browned. Remove chicken from the pan. Add onions to pan and slowly caramelize until golden brown. Set onions aside, wipe out pan and add extra-virgin olive oil. Over medium heat saute garlic until golden and lightly toasted. Add basil, sun-dried tomatoes, olives and caramelized onions. Stir together, cooking briefly. Deglaze pan with white wine and return chicken to pan, add chicken stock and simmer until chicken is cooked through and liquid is some-what reduced. Arrange chicken on a large platter with pasta mounded in the middle and sauce and veggies arranged on the pasta. Garnish with parsley if desired.

Orecchiette with Broccoli

Entree

1 pound orecchiette pasta, cooked until al dente and set aside
4 tablespoons olive oil
6 ounces sun-dried tomatoes
4 cloves garlic, finely minced
1 pound broccoli florets, par-boiled until crisp-tender
1/4 cup fresh basil leaves, chopped
1 cup canned condensed chicken broth (or 2 cups regular strength chicken broth reduced to 1 cup)
1/4 cup garlic butter (soften butter and blend with two cloves minced garlic)
1/2 cup Parmesan and Romano cheeses, shredded

Add olive oil to a skillet and heat to medium. Saute sun-dried tomatoes, garlic, broccoli and basil until garlic begins to turn golden brown. Add chicken broth and bring to boil. Place pasta in a serving bowl, add pan contents, garlic butter and cheese and toss.

*Beverage recomendation with these recipes - Castello D'Albola Chianti Classico

Vagara Bistro

Peter Hoefler
Former Chef-Owner

With its charming patio and European flair, Vagara Bistro appeals to diners seeking a sophisticated yet comfortable experience. From the warm lighting and cushy banquettes to the elegantly set tables and attentive service, this restaurant has it all. But it is more than just a pretty face, it is also a labor of love.

Co-owner Lori Hoefler runs the front of the restaurant while her husband Peter heads up the kitchen. The recipient of rigorous classic culinary training, Chef Hoefler has worked in topflight restaurants and hotels around the world.

This international background gave rise to Hoeflers distinctive cross-cultural style which is reflected in such dishes as Oriental barbecued salmon, spicy squid salad and pepper seared Chilean sea bass.

When they are not taking care of their customers, the Hoeflers enjoy boating and cooking together with their daughters Jenna and Katie.

Vagara Bistro: 6137 N. Scottsdale Rd., Scottsdale.
948-9928
(Call for reservations and hours of business.)

Spicy Seared Soft Shell Crab and Watercress Salad

Salad

Crab

4 jumbo soft shell crabs, cleaned
2 tablespoons worcestershire
1 tablespoon lemon juice
5 tablespoons flour

1/4 teaspoon cayenne
1 teaspoon paprika
salt and pepper to taste

Sprinkle crabs with lemon juice and worcestershire. In bag, combine flour, cayenne, salt and pepper and paprika and dredge crabs. Set aside.

Salad dressing

1/4 cup rice wine vinegar
2 tablespoons sesame seeds, toasted
1/2 tablespoon ground ginger
1 tablespoon sugar
1/2 teaspoon garlic, minced

1/8 cup mirin
1/4 cup orange juice
1/2 cup vegetable stock
1 tablespoon chicken stock

In medium bowl, whisk all ingredients together. Set aside.

(continued on page 153)

Five Spice Loin of Rabbit with Spicy Eggplant Stew, Black Bean Sauce and Sweet Potato Tempura

Entree

Rabbit

3 - 5 pound rabbit saddle and deboned loin with belly flap attached (available at A.J.'s)
3 or 4 hind legs, deboned with meat minced
1/2 cup shrimp, cooked and minced
1 tablespoon green onion, chopped

1 teaspoon ground ginger
salt and pepper to taste
1/2 teaspoon five spice powder
   (available at Oriental markets)
2 tablespoons peanut oil

Place rabbit loin on plastic wrap and spread belly flap. Combine minced rabbit, minced shrimp, green onion, ginger and salt and pepper. Sprinkle five spice powder on rabbit and spread minced meat mixture on the flap, rolling the loins together like a sausage and tie with string. Season outside of rabbit with five spice, salt and pepper. Heat peanut oil in skillet, sear all sides of rabbit roll and set aside.

Spicy Eggplant Stew

1/2 cup peanut oil
3 medium eggplant, in 1 inch dice
1 tablespoon garlic, finely chopped
1 teaspoon fresh ginger, finely chopped
1 tablespoon chile paste
   (available in Oriental markets)

1 tablespoon sugar
2 tablespoons soy sauce
1/4 cup strong chicken stock
3 tablespoons green onion, chopped
1/2 teaspoon sesame seeds

148

(continued on page 154)

Curried Lobster Risotto with Leek

Entree

Chef Hoefler stresses that parmesan cheese should NOT be served with this since curry and cheese are not a flavor match.

Lobster

2 2 1/2 pound lobsters
1 1/2 gallon water
1 tablespoon salt
1/2 cup peanut oil
5 stalks celery, coarsely chopped
1 leek, coarsely chopped
1 onion, coarsely chopped

piece orange peel
2 cups white wine
4 bay leaves
1 teaspoon caraway seeds
2 tablespoons ginger, coarsely chopped
1/2 gallon water
salt and pepper to taste

Boil the lobster in salted water for 5-6 minutes. Let cool slightly. Break meat from shells and set aside. Chop up lobster shells. In large pot heat peanut oil and add chopped lobster shells, celery, leek, onion and orange peel with white wine. Cook until wine has completely evaporated. Add seasonings and water to pot, bring to a boil and simmer until reduced by half. Strain and season broth to taste, bring to a boil. Prepare rice.

Risotto

2 tablespoons butter
4 shallots, finely chopped
2 pieces leek, white part only,
   1 piece chopped - 1 piece julienned
2 tablespoons curry powder

2 cups arborio rice
1/2 cup white wine
8 cups lobster broth

In medium saucepan melt butter. Add shallots and saute 2 minutes, then add chopped leek and saute 2 more minutes. Add curry powder and rice. Combine thoroughly and add white wine. Cook, stirring constantly until liquid is absorbed. Add lobster broth 1/2 cup at a time, stirring until absorbed. Continue until risotto is soft. Add butter and season to taste. Divide risotto between 4 plates with a half lobster tail and claw atop each. If desired, deep fry julienned leek and put on top of lobster.

*Beverage recommendation - Chardonnay.

Fruit Sushi with Almond Wasabi and Ruby Red Plum Sauce

Dessert

1 cup glutinous rice (available at
   Oriental markets)
1 cup water
3/4 cup coconut milk
small piece orange zest
3 tablespoons plum wine
1 teaspoon sugar

1 kiwi, peeled and sliced
kumquats in syrup (available in
   supermarket gourmet section)
pint strawberries, hulled and halved
1 mango, peeled, seeded and sliced
plum sauce (see recipe below)
almond wasabi (see recipe below)

Plum Sauce

1 pound red plums, pitted and quartered
5 tablespoons port wine
5 tablespoons orange juice

3 tablespoons honey
3 tablespoons mirin (available at
   Oriental markets)
1/2 teaspoon ground ginger

(continued on page 154)

149

Doctor Bombay's Calcutta Feast (continued-page 13)

Grilled Asparagus, Yellow Squash and Portobello Mushrooms
1/2 cup olive oil
2 garlic cloves, minced
1/4 cup cilantro, chopped
1 bunch asparagus, peeled and trimmed, blanched for 2 minutes
    and shocked in ice
2 yellow squash , sliced lengthwise into 1/4 inch sticks
2 portobello mushrooms, stems and gills removed and cut into 2 inch sticks
salt and pepper to taste

Prepare barbecue. Toss olive oil, cilantro, vegetables and seasonings together in a bowl, making sure vegetables are well-coated. Starting with the squash and mushrooms, place on grill until fully cooked. Asparagus needs just to warm up and attain some grill marks.

Assembly
Divide lentils between 4 plates, placing just off center. Top with grilled veggies and place stuffed tomato to the side.

*Beverage recomendation - Indian beer such as Golden Eagle or Kingfisher.

Grilled Lamb Saddle (continued –page 37)

1 large artichoke stem attached,
    cooked until tender
1 zucchini, thinly sliced and blanched

1 tablespoon butter
1 tablespoon garlic, minced
1 tablespoon parsley, minced

Assembly
Lay the lamb saddle flat on the back and fill cavity side with garlic, rosemary and black pepper. Roll the lamb tightly and tie with butcher string leaving 1 1/2 inches between each knot. Place lamb in the marinade and refrigerate for 24 hours. Remove from marinade and slice meat between each knot. Slices should be 1 1/2 inches thick. Prepare barbecue and grill to desired temperature. Peel leaves from artichoke and remove choke until only the heart and stem remains. Cut into quarters. Heat skillet and add butter, garlic, parsley, artichoke quarters, zucchini, salt and pepper. Stir constantly until warmed through.

Placed grilled lamb slices on warm platter with vegetables next to it and serve.

*Beverage recommendation - Story Brook "Howell Mountain", Napa red Zinfandel.

Shrimp Creole (continued –page 46)

Combine all ingredients in a bowl. Heat saucepan on high. All at once, pour ingredients into the pan and cook until tomatoes are plump and skin peels away. Remove from heat and cool.

Assembly
Divide rice on four plates. Arrange shrimp, tails up on rice and pour butter and onion sauce over. Garnish with Creole sauce.

*Beverage recommendation - Coudelet De Beaucastel.

Holiday Gingerbread House (continued—page 49)

Dessert

Preheat oven to 350°. Beat the butter and sugar together in a mixing bowl. Add eggs, molasses and vinegar and mix. Add flour, baking soda and seasonings and combine thoroughly. On floured surface, roll out to 1/4 inch thickness. Place patterns on dough and cut with a sharp knife. Place smaller pieces on one cookie sheet, larger on another. Bake 10 - 12 minuters for larger pieces, 6 - 8 minutes for smaller. Let cool.

Royal icing

1 1/2 tablespoons cream of tartar
5 egg whites
1 1/2 pound powdered sugar

In a large bowl, whip ingredients together. If desired, divide icing and tint with food colors.

Assembly

Glue the house together with the icing and decorate as desired.

*Beverage recommendation - hot chocolate.

Chayote Squash and Carrot Cake with Ancho ChileHoney (continued —page 57)

Dessert

1 1/2 cups chayote squash, peeled and grated
1 1/2 cups carrots, grated
1 cup sugar
2 eggs
3/4 cup corn oil
1 cup flour
1 teaspoon baking powder
1 teaspoon baking soda
1 teaspoon cinnamon
pinch of salt
1 teaspoon vanilla extract
1/2 cup dried cranberries
1/2 cup pistachio nuts, broken

Preheat oven to 350° F. Butter sides of bread loaf pan, line the bottom with wax paper and lightly flour. Shake out excess. Beat sugar and eggs until thickened. Beat in the oil gradually. Sift together flour, baking powder, baking soda, cinnamon and salt. Stir into egg mixture. Add the vanilla. Fold in squash, carrots, cranberries and pistachios. Spoon batter into prepared pan. Bake 35-40 minutes. Remove and cool on a wire rack.

Ancho Chile Honey

1 cup honey
1 tablespoon sugar
1 tablespoon ancho chiles, chopped
1 teaspoon fresh mint, chopped

Combine ingredients and set aside.

Slice chayote cake and place on plate. Drizzle honey over and around cake onto plate. Garnish with sprigs of mint, dried cranberries and pistachio.

*Beverage recommendation - Quady Essencia.

Herb Crusted Tournedos of Beef with Shiitake & Portobello Mushroom Ragout (cont.-pg 105)

Garlic and Herb Crouton Rounds

8 slices sourdough bread
1/4 cup melted butter
2 tablespoons garlic, minced
2 tablespoons basil

Preheat broiler. Trim crust from bread. With round cutter, cut center out of the bread. Brush rounds with butter and sprinkle with garlic and basil. Broil until golden. Set aside.

Assembly

Put two croutons on each heated plate. Place a tournedos on each crouton. Spoon ragout over middle of each tournedo. Garnish with fresh thyme if desired.

*Beverage recommendation - Murphy Merlot (Markham Vineyards).

Heirloom Potato Strudel
with Shiitake Cabernet Sauce (continued –page 128)

Shiitake Cabernet Sauce

1/4 pound shiitake mushrooms
1/4 pound shallots, peeled and chopped
1 teaspoon garlic, chopped
2 tablespoons olive oil
teaspoon black peppercorns

bundle fresh thyme
2 bay leaves
2 cups cabernet sauvignon
2 cups chicken demi-glace (see recipe below)

Preheat oven 375° Toss together mushrooms, shallots, garlic and olive oil. Place in shallow roasting pan and bake about 15 minutes or until very aromatic and golden brown. Transfer to a pot and add a bouquet garni of peppercorns, thyme and bay leaves. Add the wine and reduce completely. Add the chicken demi glace and reduce until sauce coats back of a spoon. Strain.

Chicken Demi Glace

2 pound chicken carcass, roasted to
    deep brown
8 cups water
3 sprigs thyme
1 bay leaf

2 onions, chopped
10 sprigs cilantro
3 sprigs parsley
1/4 teaspoon salt
1 tablespoon black pepper

Place all ingredients in a large pot. Bring to a boil and simmer 3 - 4 hours. Skim when necessary. Strain, return to pot and reduce to 2 cups.

Assembly

Cut strudel triangles in half, place 4 pieces on each plate with 2 pieces laying on the side and the other 2 propped up exposing the filling. Ladle sauce over top and garnish with fresh thyme if desired. (Leftover strudels freeze well. Wrap individually and thaw in refrigerator.)

*Beverage recommendation - Pinot Noir.

Snapper with Herb Broth and Mushroom
Mashed Potatoes (continued –page 129)

Snapper

4 7-ounce portions of skin-on snapper filets
2 tablespoons olive oil
2 tablespoons garlic powder
1 tablespoon onion powder
1 tablespoon dried oregano
2 tablespoons salt
1 tablespoon black pepper
1 tablespoon cayenne
1 tablespoon dried thyme

Combine all dry seasoning and lightly dust over filets (place any leftover seasoning in a bottle for future use). Heat olive oil in skillet and saute fish until opaque and firm.

Assembly

Place a spoonful of mashed potatoes in the center of 4 deep plates.
and arrange sauteed fish skin side up on top.
Carefully ladle broth around potatoes. Garnish with fresh herbs if desired.

*Beverage recommendation - Pinot Grigio.

Spicy Seared Soft Shell Crab and Watercress Salad (continued- page 148)

Watercress Salad
1 bunch watercress, leaves removed
1 cup fresh bean sprouts
1/2 cup each red and green bell pepper, julienned
1/2 cup shiitake mushrooms, sliced
1/2 cup carrots, julienned
1 Japanese or hot house cucumber, peeled and seeded, half sliced and julienned

In large bowl toss salad ingredients together. Refrigerate.

Sesame Chopsticks
1 sheet frozen puff pastry
1 egg yolk
4 tablespoons milk
1 tablespoon each black and white sesame seeds
pinch cayenne pepper

Preheat oven to 425° Lay out sheet of puff pastry. Combine egg and milk and brush on sheet. Combine seeds with cayenne and sprinkle evenly over sheet. Cut into 8 1/4-inch strips and lay on cookie sheet. Bake 35 minutes until golden brown. Set aside.

Lemon Pepper Sauce
1 potato, unpeeled, boiled and cooled slightly
1 red pepper charred over grill, sweated, peeled and deseeded
juice of 1/2 lemon
3/4 cup chicken stock
1/4 teaspoon cayenne pepper
1/2 cup olive or peanut oil
salt and pepper to taste

Peel potato. Place potato, pepper, lemon juice, chicken stock, cayenne and salt and pepper in a blender, Slowly pour in oil until mixture emulsifies. Adjust seasonings.

Assembly
Heat olive or peanut oil in deep skillet until very hot. Quickly pan fry crabs until crisp. Drain on paper towels. Toss watercress salad with dressing to taste. Divide salad between 4 plates and top each with a crab. Drizzle lemon pepper sauce around salads and lay 2 sesame chopsticks on side of each plate. Serve immediately.

*Beverage recommendation - Fume Blanc.

153

Five Spice Loin of Rabbit with Spicy Eggplant Stew, Black Bean Sauce and Sweet Potato Tempura (continued –page148)

Heat peanut oil in skillet until very hot. Fry eggplant 2 - 3 minutes. Take out of pan and place on paper towel, squeeze lightly to remove excess oil and water. Wipe out skillet and add garlic, onion, ginger, chile paste, sugar, soy and stock. Bring to a boil and add eggplant. Cook until sauce turns into a glaze. Set aside. (When dishing up later, garnish with green onion and sesame seeds.)

Black Bean Sauce

3 cups mirin (sweet Sake)1 cup soy sauce
1 teaspoon fresh ginger, finely chopped
cornstarch as needed
3 tablespoons fermented black beans
  (available at Oriental markets)

1/2 teaspoon red pepper flakes
3 tablespoons butter
4 tablespoons lemon juice

In saucepan bring mirin to a boil and reduce by half. Add soy and ginger. Thicken slightly with cornstarch. Remove from heat and add beans, pepper flakes, butter and lemon juice and mix well. Set aside.

Sweet Potato Tempura

1 small sweet potato, peeled and cut
  into 3 inch long spaghetti-sized strips
4 long strips green onion for tying
  potato bundles

1 cup all purpose flour
5 - 6 tablespoons club soda
salt and pepper
oil for deep frying

Divide potato strips in 4 bundles. Tie each in a fan with onion strip. Dust with flour. In bowl mix rest of flour, soda and seasoning, don't overmix. Dip sweet potato fans in batter and shake lightly to get rid of excess batter. Deepfry at 350°.

Assembly

After stew, sauce and tempura are prepared, preheat oven to 425° and bake rabbit loin about 4 - 6 minutes. Take off string and slice into 8 pieces. Divide eggplant stew between 4 plates, sprinkle with onions and sesame seeds. Place two slices rabbit on top. Drizzle with black bean sauce and top with sweet potato tempura.

*Beverage recommendation - Pinot Noir.

Fruit Sushi with Almond Wasabi and Ruby Red Plum Sauce (continued –page 149)

Combine all ingredients in a small sauce pot, bring to a boil and simmer until plums are tender. Put in a blender, puree, strain and set aside.

Almond Wasabi

3 tablespoons almond paste
1 - 2 drops green food coloring

Mix together well. Set aside.

Assembly

Preheat oven to 375 ° Put rice in a strainer and run cold water over it until water is clear rather than milky. Drain, place in a saucepan and add water, coconut milk and orange zest. Bring to a rapid boil for 2 minutes. Cover pan and place in oven for 30 minutes or until all liquid is absorbed. Remove from oven. Dissolve sugar in plum wine and pour over rice. Cool. Form rice as for sushi in palm of hand, squaring with other hand. Place sliced fruit atop rice. Arrange on a platter with almond wasabi and serve with dipping sauce.

*Beverage recommendation - plum wine.

Chef Patrick Hughes, Old Town Tortilla Factory

Prickly pear cactus, an ingredient common to Mexicans and Native Americans is often mistaken by Arizonans as just part of the scenery. Known as nopales in Spanish, the cactus has a wide variety of uses. The pad can be used as a vegetable and the fruit, or prickly pear, is used in desserts and sauces. This dish has regional Mexican influence as well as Native American. Mixit is a Cherokee dish using a bounty of summer vegetables that is very similar to ratatouille.

12 jumbo prawns, peeled and deveined
chipotle prickly pear sauce (see recipe below)
nopales mixit (see recipe below)
radishes and lime slices (garnish)

Chipotle Prickly Pear Sauce

6 prickly pears, diced
1 tablespoon olive oil
1 cup onion, diced
2 tablespoons garlic, minced
6 tomatoes, roasted, peeled and crushed

3 chipotle peppers in adobo sauce
3 teaspoons of adobo sauce from can
3 cups chicken stock
salt and pepper to taste

Heat olive oil in a skillet and saute onions and garlic about 6 - 8 minutes. Add the tomatoes, chipotles, sauce and chicken stock. Reduce by 1/3 over medium heat. Add prickly pear fruit and simmer 5 minutes. Remove from heat and blenderize until liquified. Adjust seasonings and set aside.

Nopales Mixit

8 cactus pads (available at Southwest supermarkets or your own yard) or, you may substitute prepared, bottled nopalitos (drain and rinse)
2 tablespoons olive oil
2 cups onion, diced
2 tablespoons garlic, minced
2 1/2 cups corn, roasted and removed from cob
1/2 cup white tequila
1 1/2 pounds tomatoes, roasted, peeled and crushed
1/3 cilantro leaves, chopped
salt and pepper to taste

Trim 1/4 inch off the edge of each cactus pad, lay pad flat and remove all spines. Cut the pad into 1/2 inch squares, put in a sauce pan, cover with water and boil for 12 minutes. Remove from heat and drain, rinsing first with hot water then cold to remove the viscosity. Set aside. Meanwhile, heat oil in a skillet and saute the onions and garlic until onions are slightly browned. Add corn and saute 3 more minutes. Remove pan from heat and deglaze with the tequila. Add tomatoes and reserved nopales and cook 5 minutes, season to taste.

Assembly

Grill or pan sear shrimp until just done (don't overcook). Place 3 shrimp, nopales mixit and sauce on each plate and garnish with sliced radishes and lime slices.

L

Lagniappe Salad with Blue Cheese Dressing 28
Lamb:
    Chops, Mesquite Grilled with Thai Peanut
        Sauce and Kettle Chips 121
    Saddle, Grilled 37
    Tenderloin with Spring Vegetables
        and Brown Rice 140
Lemon Dill Marinated Salmon
    over Angel Hair Fritatta 17

M

Malaysian Shrimp 25
Manchego Filet 52
Medaglion Di Vitello Alla Panna (Veal Medallion
    in Cream Sauce) 113
Mesquite Grilled Lamb Chops with Thai Peanut
    Sauce and Kettle Chips 121
Mixed Greens Salad with Raspberry
    Vinaigrette 124
Mostaccioli with Broccoli and Sundried
    Tomatoes 101

O

Okra and Sweet Corn Gumbo with Buttered
    Squash Timbales 128
Orange Segment and Spicy Walnut Salad 16
Orange Tree's Chocolate Spire 53
Orecchiette with Broccoli 145
Oysters Michelina 100

P

Pan-Seared Duck on a Rosemary Pancake with
    Wilted Greens and Dried Berry Relish 120
Pan-Seared Pistachio Crusted Halibut with
    Strawberry Chile Compote a la Navajo 49
Pan-Seared Salmon with a Light Herb
    Horseradish Crust and Mango Vinaigrette 120
Panzarotti Joey Bistro (Potato Cheese
    Croquette) 136
Pasta:
    Angel Hair Frittata 17
    Angel Hair with Tomato Fennel Sauce 124
    Chicken Siciliano 145
    Key West Shrimp with Sweet Vegetable
        Saute and Angel Hair 60
    Mostaccioli with Broccoli and Sundried
        Tomatoes 101
    Orecchiette with Broccoli 145
    Penne Arrabiata 24
    Penne Salsa Cruda 69
    Red Snapper with Clams and Mussels
        over Linguine 100

Sprouts Sedona Sunset Shrimp with
    Lemon Pepper Pasta 48
Pasta E' Fagioli Soup 20
Pea and Curry Soup 36
Peach Cobbler with Pecan and Cornmeal
    Crust 109
Penne Arrabiata 24
Penne Salsa Cruda 69
Pepita-Crusted Crab Cakes with Chipotle Aioli 88
Pollo Tampiqueno 109
Pork:
    Barbequed Pork and Eggplant Wrap
        with Mixed Greens 133
    Barbequed Ribs 33
    Chops and Cherry Peppers 125
    Jamaican Barbecue Tenderloin with Mango
        Sour Cherry Compote 105
    Loin Crusted with Cracked Black
        Peppercorn and Pommery Mustard 12
    Tenderloin Marinated in Dark Beer with
        Candied Nectarine and Onion Sauce and
        Creamy Yellow Grits 56
    Tenderloin with Roasted Tomatoes and
        Fennel Celeriac Slaw 137
    Tenderloin with Smoked Four Onion Relish
        and Sweet Potato Cakes 141
    Tinga Poblana 108
Potato and Cheese Enchiladas 85
Poultry:
    Chicken Fricassee 37
    Chicken Piccata 21
    Chicken Salad with Roasted Pecans, Celery,
        Jicama and Dates 84
    Chicken Siciliano 145
    Chicken Vesuvio 68
    Chopped Chicken Salad 144
    Coq au Vin 45
    Crepes Two Ways with Chicken Breast Filling 40
    Crostini 64
    Jambalaya 29
    Pan Seared Duck on a Rosemary Pancake
        with Wilted Greens and Dried Berry
        Relish 120
    Penne Arrabiata 24
    Pollo Tampiqueno 109
    Raspberry Chipotle Glazed Duck Breast
        with Carrot Jalapeno Mousse 76
    Roast Duck with Sundried Cranberry
        and Walnut Cabernet Sauce 61
    Stuffed Chicken in Phyllo with Asparagus
        and Tomatoes 117
Provencal Pot Roast 89

Q

Quenelles; Arborio Rice, Goat Cheese &
    Sun-dried Tomatoes with Port Wine Glaze 16

Enchilada for spinach 97
Enchilada for Vegi-ladas 97
Herb Broth for Snapper 129
Lemon Pepper for Spicy Seared Soft
  Shell Crab 148
Lemon Yogurt Mint for Lamb
  Tenderloin 140
Mango Vinaigrette for Pan Seared
  Salmon 120
Marsala Wine for Veal 21
Papaya Salsa 116
Parmesan Cream for Mushroom Risotto
  Cakes with Seafood 60
Peach Rosemary Salsa 137
Poblano Cream 85
Pommery Mustard 12
Remoulade 28
Roasted Garlic Barbecue Glaze for
  Scottsdale Mixed Grill 121
Ruby Red Plum for Fruit Sushi 149
Salsa Verde for Pork Tenderloin 141
Sauce for Lemon Dill Marinated Salmon 17
Sauce for Oysters Michelina 100
Shiitake Cabernet for Heirloom Potato
  Strudel 128
Smoked Tomato 17
Sundried Cranberry and Walnut Cabernet
  for Roast Duck 61
Sweet Chile 89
Tangy Plum Ketchup 57
Thai Peanut 121
Vanilla Bean for Indian Pudding 117
Wasabi Cream 76
Wheat Beer Aioli 76
Yogurt Cucumber Mint 25
Sauteed Scallop Salad with Baby Breens and
  Citrus Vinaigrette 88
Scottsdale Mixed Grill 121

SEAFOOD:
Ahi Tuna with Mango Chile Chutney 53
Arselle E Peoci Umido (Stewed Mussels
  and Clams) 112
Baja Dorado Fish Tacos 92
Calamari Con Piselli All' Anconetana (Squid
  and Peas Ancona Style) 113
Chaparral's World Famous Lobster Bisque 48
Crispy Prawn and Basil Wonton Salad
  with Papaya Fruit Salsa and Citrus
  Ginger Dressing 116
Curried Lobster Risotto with Leek 149
Fresh Fried Catfish 104
Gumbo 44
Jambalaya 29
Oysters Michelina 100

Pan Seared Pistachio Crusted Halibut with
  Strawberry Chile Compote a la Navajo 49
Pepita-Crusted Crab Cakes with Chipotle
  Aioli 88
Red Snapper with Clams and Mussels
  over Linguine 100
Red Snapper en Papillotte 41
Salmon au jus de Carotte 41
Salmon, Lemon Dill Marinated over Angel
  Hair Fritatta 17
Salmon, Pan Seared with Light Herb
  Horseradish Crust and Mango
  Vinaigrette 120
Salmon and Shrimp Mousse Potstickers
  with Gingered Mashed Potatoes and
  Plum Sauce 77
Sauteed Scallop Salad with Baby Greens
  and Citrus Vinaigrette 88
Scottsdale Mixed Grill (shrimp) 121
Sesame Seared Ahi with Wheat Beer Aioli
  and Wasabi Cream 76
Shrimp and Roasted Corn Soup 84
Shrimp, Bill Johnson's Barbecued 32
Shrimp, Cajun Barbecued 29
Shrimp Creole 45
Shrimp, Key West with Sweet Vegetable
  Saute 60
Shrimp, Malaysian 25
Shrimp Remoulade 28
Shrimp, Sprouts Sedona Sunset 48
Snapper with Herb Broth and Mushroom
  Mashed Potatoes 129
Sonoran Spring Roll 52
Southwest Shrimp Caesar Salad 132
Spicy Seared Soft Shell Crab
  with Watercress Salad 148
Stuffed Mushrooms 20
Wild Mushroom Risotto Cakes
  with Seafood in Parmesan Cream
  Sauce 60
Sesame Bananas 81
Sesame Seared Ahi with Wheat Beel Aioli and
  Wasabi Cream 76
Shrimp and Roasted Corn Soup 84
Shrimp, Bill Johnson's Barbecued 32
Shrimp, Cajun Barbecued 29
Shrimp Creole 45
Shrimp, Key West with Sweet Vegetable
  Saute 60
Shrimp, Malaysian 25
Shrimp Remoulade 28
Skillet Apple Pie ala Mode 93
Smoked Corn and Sunflower Sprout Soup 108
Snapper with Herb Broth and Mushroom
  Mashed Potatoes 129
Sonoran Spring Roll 52

SOUPS:

Albondigas 92
Butternut Squash with Pasilla Chiles 56
Chaparral's World Famous Lobster Bisque 48
Gazpacho 132
Okra and Sweet Corn Gumbo with Buttered
  Squash Timbales 128
Pasta E' Fagioli (Pasta and Beans) 20
Pea and Curry 36
Seafood Gumbo 44
Shrimp and Roasted Corn 84
Smoked Corn and Sunflower Sprout 108
Stracciatella 68
Tortilla 97
Southwest Marinated Flank Steak 73
Southwest Shrimp Caesar Salad 132
Spicy Beef Salad 136
Spicy Seared Soft Shell Crab and Watercress
  Salad 148
Spinach-Artichoke Cheese Dip 144
Spinach Enchiladas 96
Sprouts Sedona Sunset Shrimp with Lemon
  Pepper Pasta 48
Stracciatella 68
Stuffed Chicken in Phyllo with Asparagus
  and Tomatoes 117

T

Tiramisu 101
Tenderloin Tower with Smoked Tomato
  Sauce 17
Tinga Poblana (Pork Stew) 108
Tomato Towers with Yogurt Cucumber Mint
  Sauce 25
Torta di Riso e Nocciole (Rice and Hazelnut
  Cake) 65
Tortilla Soup 97

V

Veal Chop Mostarda 64
Veal Chop with Peach Rosemary Salsa 137
Veal Marsala 21
Veal Vogherese 69
Vegetable Chilaquiles Casserole 72
Vegetable(s):
  Buttered Squash Timbales (with Okra and
    Sweet Corn Gumbo) 128
  Carrot Jalapeno Mousse 76
  Corn and Red Onion Relish 57
  Creamy Yellow Grits 56
  Crepes Two Ways with Ratatouille 40

Doctor Bombay's Calcutta Feast (Basmati
  stuffed tomatoes with grilled asparagus,
  yellow squash & Portobello mushrooms
  on braised lentil ragout) 13
Far East Avocado Dip with Parsnip and
  Sweet Potato Chips 24
Parsnip Chips 24
Potatoes:
  and Cheese Enchiladas 85
  and Cheese Croquette 13
  au Gratin 57
  Ginger Mashed 77
  Gnocchi 37
  Kettle Chips 121
  and Smoked Cheddar au Gratin 57
  Heirloom Strudel with Shiitake Cabernet
    Sauce 128
  Mushroom Mashed 129
  Sweet Cakes 141
  Sweet Chips 24
  Sweet Tempura 148
  Potato and Cheese Enchiladas
  Potato Gnocchi 37
Red Beans and Rice 44
Spicy Eggplant Stew 148
Spinach Enchiladas 96
Tomato Tower with Yogurt Cucumber
  Mint Sauce 25
Vegetable Chilaquiles Casserole 72
Vegetarian Spring Rolls 80
Vegi-ladas 97

W

Warm Blueberry Tart with Ginger Ice
  Cream 129
Wedge of Iceberg with Cool Blue
  Dressing, A 140
Western Chili 32
Wild Mushroom Risotto Cakes with Seafood
  in Parmesan Cream Sauce 60
Wokked 5-Spice Beef and Rice Noodles with
  Sweet Chile Sauce 89

GIFT CERTIFICATE

A.J.'s

7141 E. Lincoln Dr., Scottsdale 998-0052 · 10105 E. ViaLinda, Scottsdale 391-9863
5017 N. Central Ave., Phoenix 230-7015 · 13226 N. 7th Street, Phoenix, 863-3500
23251 N. Pima Rd., Scottsdale, 563-5070

AMOUNT $10

GIFT CERTIFICATE

ALDO BALDO

7014 E. Camelback Rd., (Scottsdale Fashion Square), Scottsdale
994-0062

AMOUNT $10

GIFT CERTIFICATE

ANZIO LANDING
ITALIAN RESTAURANT

S.W. Corner of Higley & McDowell (Falcon Field Airport), Mesa
832-1188

AMOUNT $10

GIFT CERTIFICATE

ARMADILLO GRILL

1904 E. Camelback Rd., Phoenix
287-0700

AMOUNT $10

GIFT CERTIFICATE

BABY KAY'S CAJUN KITCHEN

7216 E. Shoeman Lane, Scottsdale 990-9080
2119 E. Camelback Rd. (Town & Country Village), Phoenix 955-0011

$10 $10 AMOUNT $10 $10 $10

GIFT CERTIFICATE

BILL JOHNSON'S BIG APPLE

3757 E. Van Buren St. ,Phoenix 275-2107 · 3101 W. Indian School Rd., Phoenix 277-6291
16810 N. 19th Ave., Phoenix 863-7921 · 950 E. Main St., Mesa 969-6504
3110 N. Arizona Ave., Chandler 892-2542

$10 $10 AMOUNT $10 $10 $10

GIFT CERTIFICATE

BISTRO 24
THE RITZ-CARLTON, PHOENIX

2401 E. Camelback Rd. Phoenix
952-2424

$10 $10 AMOUNT $10 $10 $10

GIFT CERTIFICATE

Marriott's CAMELBACK INN

5402 E. Lincoln Dr., Scottsdale
948-1700

$10 $10 AMOUNT $10 $10 $10

GIFT CERTIFICATE

CAPERS
ORANGE TREE GOLF & CONFERENCE RESORT

10601 N. 56th Street, Scottsdale
443-2119

AMOUNT $10

GIFT CERTIFICATE

DRINKWATER'S

8711 E. Pinnacle Peak Rd., Scottsdale
998-2222

AMOUNT $10

GIFT CERTIFICATE

GIANNI

10155 E. ViaLinda, Scottsdale
657-0818

AMOUNT $10

GIFT CERTIFICATE

GRIFF'S
AT MERV GRIFFIN'S WICKENBURG INN

8 miles north of Wickenburg on State Route 89 (Prescott Highway)
1-800-WICKENBURG

AMOUNT $10

GIFT CERTIFICATE

CAPERS
ORANGE TREE GOLF & CONFERENCE RESORT

10601 N. 56th Street, Scottsdale
443-2119

One certificate per visit, per couple. Not valid with any other offer or on holidays.
EXPIRATION DATE: DECEMBER 30, 1998

GIFT CERTIFICATE

DRINKWATER'S

8711 E. Pinnacle Peak Rd., Scottsdale
998-2222

One certificate per visit, per couple. Not valid with any other offer or on holidays.
EXPIRATION DATE: DECEMBER 30, 1998

GIFT CERTIFICATE

GIANNI

10155 E. ViaLinda, Scottsdale
657-0818

One certificate per visit, per couple. Not valid with any other offer or on holidays.
EXPIRATION DATE: DECEMBER 30, 1998

GIFT CERTIFICATE

GRIFF'S
AT MERV GRIFFIN'S WICKENBURG INN

8 miles north of Wickenburg on State Route 89 (Prescott Highway)
1-800-WICKENBURG

One certificate per visit, per couple. Not valid with any other offer or on holidays.
EXPIRATION DATE: DECEMBER 30, 1998

GIFT CERTIFICATE

HOPS! BISTRO & BREWERY

2584 E. Camelback Rd. (Biltmore Fashion Park), Phoenix 468-0500
8668 E. Shea Blvd., Scottsdale 998-7777

AMOUNT $10

GIFT CERTIFICATE

JADE PALACE

9160 E. Shea Blvd., Scottsdale
391-0607

AMOUNT $10

GIFT CERTIFICATE

LA TÂCHE
WORLD BISTRO & WINE BAR

4175 Goldwater Blvd., Scottsdale
946-0377

AMOUNT $10

GIFT CERTIFICATE

MANUEL'S MEXICAN RESTAURANTS

1111 W. Bell Rd., Phoenix 993-8778 · 1123 W. Broadway Rd., Tempe 968-4437
12801 N. Cave Creek Rd., Phoenix 971-3680 · 2820 E. Indian School Rd., Phoenix 957-7540
3162 E. Indian School Rd., Phoenix 956-1120 · 5509 N. 7th St., Phoenix 274-6426
5670 W. Peoria, Glendale 979-3500 · 2350 E. Southern Ave., Tempe 897-0025

AMOUNT $10

GIFT CERTIFICATE

HOPS! BISTRO & BREWERY

2584 E. Camelback Rd. (Biltmore Fashion Park), Phoenix 468-0500
8668 E. Shea Blvd., Scottsdale 998-7777

One certificate per visit, per couple. Not valid with any other offer or on holidays.
EXPIRATION DATE: DECEMBER 30, 1998

GIFT CERTIFICATE

JADE PALACE

9160 E. Shea Blvd., Scottsdale
391-0607

One certificate per visit, per couple. Not valid with any other offer or on holidays.
EXPIRATION DATE: DECEMBER 30, 1998

GIFT CERTIFICATE

LA TÂCHE
WORLD BISTRO & WINE BAR

4175 Goldwater Blvd., Scottsdale
946-0377

One certificate per visit, per couple. Not valid with any other offer or on holidays.
EXPIRATION DATE: DECEMBER 30, 1998

GIFT CERTIFICATE

MANUEL'S MEXICAN RESTAURANTS

1111 W. Bell Rd., Phoenix 993-8778 · 1123 W. Broadway Rd., Tempe 968-4437
12801 N. Cave Creek Rd., Phoenix 971-3680 · 2820 E. Indian School Rd., Phoenix 957-7540
3162 E. Indian School Rd., Phoenix 956-1120 · 5509 N. 7th St., Phoenix 274-6426
5670 W. Peoria, Glendale 979-3500 · 2350 E. Southern Ave., Tempe 897-0025

One certificate per visit, per couple. Not valid with any other offer or on holidays.
EXPIRATION DATE: DECEMBER 30, 1998

GIFT CERTIFICATE

MARILYN'S
FIRST MEXICAN RESTAURANT

12631 N. Tatum Blvd., Phoenix
953-2121

AMOUNT $10

GIFT CERTIFICATE

MICHELINA'S

3241 E Shea Blvd., Phoenix
996-8977

AMOUNT $10

GIFT CERTIFICATE

OLD TOWN TORTILLA FACTORY

6910 E. Main Street, Scottsdale
945-4567

AMOUNT $10

GIFT CERTIFICATE

PANE e VINO

8900 E. Pinnacle Peak Rd., Suite D-1, Scottsdale
473-7900

AMOUNT $10

GIFT CERTIFICATE

MARILYN'S
FIRST MEXICAN RESTAURANT

12631 N. Tatum Blvd., Phoenix
953-2121

$10 $10 $10 $10 $10

One certificate per visit, per couple. Not valid with any other offer or on holidays.
EXPIRATION DATE: DECEMBER 30, 1998

GIFT CERTIFICATE

MICHELINA'S

3241 E Shea Blvd., Phoenix
996-8977

$10 $10 $10 $10 $10

One certificate per visit, per couple. Not valid with any other offer or on holidays.
EXPIRATION DATE: DECEMBER 30, 1998

GIFT CERTIFICATE

OLD TOWN TORTILLA FACTORY

6910 E. Main Street, Scottsdale
945-4567

$10 $10 $10 $10 $10

One certificate per visit, per couple. Not valid with any other offer or on holidays.
EXPIRATION DATE: DECEMBER 30, 1998

GIFT CERTIFICATE

PANE e VINO

8900 E. Pinnacle Peak Rd., Suite D-1, Scottsdale
473-7900

$10 $10 $10 $10 $10

One certificate per visit, per couple. Not valid with any other offer or on holidays.
EXPIRATION DATE: DECEMBER 30, 1998

GIFT CERTIFICATE

CAFE PATOU

7000 E. Shea Blvd. (Scottsdale Promenade), Scottsdale
951-6868

$10 $10   AMOUNT $10 $10 $10

GIFT CERTIFICATE

QUILL CREEK CAFE
AT GRAYHAWK GOLF CLUB

8620 E. Thompson Peak Parkway, Scottsdale
502-1700

$10 $10   AMOUNT $10 $10 $10

GIFT CERTIFICATE

REMINGTON'S
SCOTTSDALE PLAZA RESORT
7200 N. Scottsdale Rd., Scottsdale
951-5101

$10 $10   AMOUNT $10 $10 $10

GIFT CERTIFICATE

THE ROSE RESTAURANT

234 S. Cortez, Prescott
520-777-8308

$10 $10   AMOUNT $10 $10 $10

GIFT CERTIFICATE

CAFE PATOU

7000 E. Shea Blvd. (Scottsdale Promenade), Scottsdale
951-6868

One certificate per visit, per couple. Not valid with any other offer or on holidays.
EXPIRATION DATE: DECEMBER 30, 1998

$10 $10 $10 $10 $10

GIFT CERTIFICATE

QUILL CREEK CAFE
AT GRAYHAWK GOLF CLUB

8620 E. Thompson Peak Parkway, Scottsdale
502-1700

One certificate per visit, per couple. Not valid with any other offer or on holidays.
EXPIRATION DATE: DECEMBER 30, 1998

$10 $10 $10 $10

GIFT CERTIFICATE

REMINGTON'S
SCOTTSDALE PLAZA RESORT

7200 N. Scottsdale Rd., Scottsdale
951-5101

One certificate per visit, per couple. Not valid with any other offer or on holidays.
EXPIRATION DATE: DECEMBER 30, 1998

$10 $10 $10 $10

GIFT CERTIFICATE

THE ROSE RESTAURANT

234 S. Cortez, Prescott
520-777-8308

One certificate per visit, per couple. Not valid with any other offer or on holidays.
EXPIRATION DATE: DECEMBER 30, 1998

$10 $10 $10 $10